UNDER THE SPELL

OF

HARRY POTTER

BY

STEPHEN DOLLINS

All scripture quotations are taken from the
Authorized King James Version of the Bible.

Printed in the United States of America

ISBN #1-58538-015-6

Dedication

I would like to thank my Lord Jesus Christ and my precious Heavenly Father for giving me the motivation, courage, and strength to write and finish this book. It is about a subject that it is so vitally important to have knowledge of in these days, when teachings and doctrines that are so far from the truth of God and the Bible, are being accepted and embraced.

I dedicate this book to my wife, Jo Ann, and to my daughter, Eryn. Thank you for your support, prayers, and faith in me. Thank you, Jo Ann, for sharing your time and pushing me to get this project done. I love you.

Special gratitude goes to Berit Kjos of Crossroad Ministry, Caryl Matrisciana, and other ministers and ministries who have been bold enough to expose the Harry Potter phenomenon for what it really is.

CONTENTS

UNDER THE SPELL OF HARRY POTTER

INTRODUCTION

The following statements are replies from school children after being asked what they thought about the Harry Potter books:

> "I was eager to get to Hogwart's first, because I liked what they learned there, and **I want to be a witch**." Gloria Bishop, age 10.

> "I like the third book, because here, Harry meets his godfather and Professor Lupin, a really cool guy (a shape-shifter who turns into a werewolf)." Harry Libarle, age 7.

In the Word of God, I Timothy 4:1-2 says: *"Now the Spirit speaketh expressly, that in the latter times some shall depart from the faith, giving heed to seducing spirits, and doctrines of devils; Speaking lies in hypocrisy; having their conscience seared with a hot iron."*

Being a former Satanic High Priest, I can tell you that I have seen witchcraft packaged in many clever forms, but never one as clever as the one we are about to examine. To be very blunt, **this is witchcraft in the form of a child's book!**

The character, known as Harry Potter, arose on the literary scene just before Christmas of '99. The oddest thing about this was that children were asking for the Harry Potter books more than toys! What's wrong with this picture? It seems that children were actually asking for something to read, rather than something to play with. The latest craze for children is a series of books about the life of an ordinary 11 year-old boy, whose life is changed through the magical world of witchcraft and wizardry. They are written by a female British author, J.K. Rowling, and are known as the *Harry Potter* series.

Another odd thing about this series is that it isn't just children who are rushing to get these books. Just as many adults are entertained, excited and absorbing the content of these books as they follow the story lines.

Harry Potter is the story of a young boy who discovers he's really a wizard—in other words, a sorcerer! Four books have been released in the Harry Potter series, with 3.8 million copies of the fourth book released in the United States on July 8, 2000.

Worldwide, 35 million copies of the first three books are in print, with about half of these total sales in the United States [*USA Today*, 6/22/00].

The first book, *Harry Potter and the Sorcerer's Stone*, was released in England entitled *Harry Potter and the Philosopher's Stone*. Interesting that the book released in England was given a very different book cover than the one released in the United States.

The "philosopher's stone" is a part of the lore of alchemy and medieval sorcery. It was supposedly a stone that could be used to turn base metal to gold; therefore, it was considered to be the "Holy Grail" of sorcery.

While the author has been hailed as a clever and imaginative writer whose books have gotten our children to read again, we have to realize that these stories center on a character who is learning the arts of sorcery and witchcraft. While some, including prominent Christian leaders, say these books are just innocent fantasy, one has to examine whether as Christians, we should be involved in the world of fantasy—especially if it involves the art of witchcraft. Many have argued since Harry Potter represents the fight of good vs. evil and is in the context of fantasy, that it is okay for our children to read.

We must, however, also examine this premise closely and ask these questions: "Are the sorcery and magic in Harry Potter just fantasy? Is it biblical to accept the use of 'good' magical powers if they are used to fight evil? Is there such a thing as 'good' witchcraft? Do these books present good and appropriate role models for our children and aid in teaching them the kinds of family values, morals and standards that we want them to have acquired by the time they reach adulthood?"

If we go to what our Almighty Heavenly Father has to say about the practice of magical arts, we find the following scripture to be quite clear.

INTRODUCTION

Deuteronomy 18:9-11 *"When thou art come into the land which the LORD thy God giveth thee, thou shalt not learn to do after the abominations of those nations. There shall not be found among you any one that maketh his son or his daughter to pass through the fire* [speaking of human sacrifice], *or that useth divination* [fortune-telling by ANY means], *or an observer of times* [charting one's destiny by the stars or planets as in Astrology], *or an enchanter* [one who seduces or hypnotizes others by words and chants], *or a witch. Or a charmer* [one who casts spells by the use of magical seals, symbols or charms], *or a consulter with familiar spirits* [consulting with demon spirits acting as the deceased], *or a wizard* [a male practitioner of the Black Arts], *or a necromancer* [one who summons the spirits of the dead, in order to gain knowledge from them]. "

Oops, there's strike one against Harry Potter being innocent! As we will see, Harry learns and uses almost ALL of these in the books. And what about Harry practicing "good" witchcraft? According to the Word of God, the only good witch is a "dead" witch!

Exodus 22:18 *"Thou shalt not suffer a witch to live."* [Death is the penalty for witchcraft.] STRIKE TWO!

Is there a hidden meaning and purpose to these books? Are they just innocent children's stories? **YOU** decide for yourself!

UNDER THE SPELL OF HARRY POTTER

CHAPTER ONE
SYMBOLS OF THE OCCULT

At this point, before beginning our journey into the study of this phenomenon, it is necessary to educate the reader concerning the symbols and charms used in all aspects of the occult (as you will be seeing them in the use of the Harry Potter book series).

These descriptions are to alert the reader that these symbols are NOT innocent, and the use of them on the book covers is by design— not coincidence. We will address the ones seen most often on the book covers.

Most of you will recognize this first symbol as being that which appears on the back side of our one dollar bills. It is the capstone suspended over the base of a pyramid and contains the "all-seeing eye" (of Lucifer). It represents the seal of the infamous Illuminati, a very powerful satanic organization which uses its power, influence and wealth to achieve the goal of establishing a One World Government under the leadership of the Antichrist. The **triangle** has always been a very powerful spell casting symbol, because it represents the three basic elements of universal witchcraft—earth, wind and fire—represented by the shape's three points.

Satanic "S"

The Satanic "S" is another symbol for Satan. It actually comes from the Bible where Jesus said in Luke 10:18, *"And he said unto them, I beheld Satan as lightning fall from heaven."*

Satanists quickly gravitated to this concept and said, "Excellent, we will represent our master, Satan, as a lightning bolt."

In witchcraft, many different gods and goddesses are worshipped, but the greatest and most cherished goddess is Diana. This is the **Crest of the Goddess Diana.** She is called the goddess of the moon and is represented as a crescent moon with a star, or stars. The Crest is often worn by the High Priestess of a coven of witches, showing her rank in that coven.

The **Pentagram** is the universal symbol of witchcraft. It is a five-pointed star with intersecting lines. Coven members wear this symbol as a charm or amulet around their neck, or on their person, believing that this symbol protects them from the forces they are summoning in their rituals. This symbol is also drawn or painted on the floor of the meeting room. There the coven members enter into the symbol and invoke their deities to take form, outside the lines of the magic circle.

This symbol is called an **Ankh**. It is an Egyptian symbol of the worship of the sun god, Ra. It is also the universal symbol of reincarnation. Note how, instead of a regular cross, having an extension at the top, this cross loops, symbolizing that life does not end, it just continues over and over again until the person reaches the state of "perfection". It is also a symbol of sexual fertility.

UNDER THE SPELL OF HARRY POTTER

CHAPTER TWO
A WIZARD IS BORN

*T*he Harry Potter novels, authored by Joanne K. Rowling, have met with a barrage of controversy over the past four years. They have also met with an astonishing sales response. Seventy-six million copies have been sold, and there are translations in 42 languages, with all four book titles on the current best seller list of *The New York Times*.

While most critics hail these books as presenting the world of witchcraft and sorcery in a positive manner claiming the books are essentially harmless fantasy that fill an inner need, I strongly believe these books are designed to desensitize our children and introduce them to witchcraft and wizardry—the "real" kind! What better way to induct our youth into the occult than through children's books? Remember, the cliché: Get them while they're young and you have them for life!

Keep in mind that figures such as Pokemon, Digimon, Teletubbies and Harry Potter are all designed by Satan and his human agents to "teach" something. If THEY can get the parents, the schools and the very church itself to accept them, then THEY have accomplished that task.

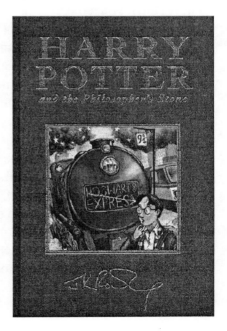

As stated in the Introduction, the first book to arrive on the market was entitled *Harry Potter and the Sorcerer's Stone*. Remember, this title was changed from the original *Harry Potter and the Philosopher's Stone*.

Note how the original book cover from England (shown on the right) differs greatly with that of the one released in the United States.

UNDER THE SPELL OF HARRY POTTER

Please examine the cover of the United States' version. Very interesting!

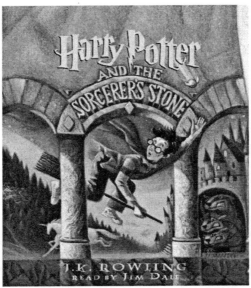

First of all, if you look at the name Harry Potter, you see that the P in Potter forms into a lightning bolt (see Occult Symbols). Harry also sports a lightning bolt scar in the middle of his forehead. Next, notice the TRIANGLE symbols on each side of the middle arch. You can also see that Harry is riding on a broomstick, one of the ancient means of travel, and a phallic symbol for witches. In the bottom right corner are "demon" dogs watching him. Harry has his **left** hand extended into the air; and on his glasses the right lens is clear, while the **left** is the color red. (In the occult, everything on the **left** symbolizes evil.) In the bottom left corner a Unicorn (symbol of enlightenment in the occult) runs wild. And what about the word "Sorcerer"? The root of this word is from the Greek word "Phar-maka", referring to a potion or drug. This is where we get the word pharmacy or pharmaceutical, meaning "to treat with drugs". In Witchcraft, it is the practice of magic through "drugs". As you can see, there are numerous hidden messages in the cover alone.

So, just who is this character, Harry Potter, and why is he such a hero to children?

Harry is a young boy who is sent to England to live with his horrible aunt and uncle, the Dursleys, after his parents are killed in a tragic "accident" while Harry is still a baby.

Harry is a nobody, who is treated like dirt by his aunt and uncle, and their wicked son, Dudley. For the first ten years of his life he sleeps under the stairs of his only living relatives, who despise him and see nothing special in him. Unbeknownst to Harry, his parents (a witch and wizard) were murdered by another evil wizard named Voldemort, chief of all the wizards who have gone too far into their practice of the "Dark Arts." Harry, for some unexplained reason, survived the attack and was rescued by other witches and wizards, who took him to a suburb of London to be raised by the Dursleys.

Then, on Harry's 11th birthday, his life changes! There is a mysterious letter delivered to the house by a Giant. This letter is an invitation to a wonderful place he never dreamed existed. Harry has been invited to come and join **Hogwart's School of Witchcraft & Wizardry**! Harry now sees himself as someone "special" and he can't think about anything other than how to get away from the Dursleys, and get to this school. So Harry does just that. After boarding a "special" train to take him there, he finds himself surrounded by wizards, witches, a white owl named "Hedwig", and jellybeans that come in every flavor imaginable.

Harry is told that he was given this invitation because the witches and wizards "knew" that Harry had been born with a special "gift" for magic. Know where he gets this gift? In the middle of Harry's forehead is a purple scar—a lightning bolt scar—that he received in the accident in which his parents were killed! The scar is the source of the power behind his psychic abilities and capacity to make magic!

At Hogwart's School, Harry meets the headmaster, Professor Dumbledore, who is the unofficial chief of all the "good" wizards worldwide. Harry makes friends with fellow students Ron and Hermione. In this first book of the series, Harry learns that the Dark Lord, Voldemort himself, is seeking to recapture his magical strength and gain control over the world. Professor Quirrel, another of Harry's instructors, is in league with Voldemort and attempts to help him gain his powers back by stealing the Sorcerer's Stone, which contains the "elixir of eternal life". If Voldemort can kill Harry, he can obtain full power. This now becomes Voldemort's goal, as Harry is the only one who has ever resisted Voldemort's curse of murder!

In the finale, Voldemort "possesses" Quirrel and lures Harry into a confrontation, attempting to kill Harry and gain possession of the stone. However, our "hero" is too strong an opponent for him; Voldemort flees, with Harry collapsing and remaining unconscious for about three days before he is revived. A "star" is born!

In the sequel to *Harry Potter and the Sorcerer's Stone*, the second book in the series called *Harry Potter and the Chamber of Secrets*, we find more Black Magic and danger. First of all, we need look no further than the cover of the book to find some more hidden messages. From the beginning of time, the enemy of God and His saints on earth, Satan, has been represented by the symbol of the snake (or serpent) as he appeared in the Garden of Eden. There are a number of serpents on the cover of this book. A huge serpent, who has blended into the column at the far right corner, lies in wait, entwined around the pole. There are green serpents awaiting our hero in the chamber, and Harry, complete with his lightning bolt scar, is holding on to a mythical bird, called the Phoenix (another symbol of reincarnation). If we look to Harry's left, on the wall, a serpent arched on a torch appears. This torch closely resembles the rounded flame, (posing as the loop at the top of the cross) and the serpent completing the cross (the **Ankh**).

The plot begins by describing Harry's horrible summer with his aunt and uncle and the rest of the Dursely family, who despise him. His attempt to hop a train back to the school to begin his second year in training is thwarted, but that is nothing compared to what awaits him within the haunted walls of Hogwart's! The mysterious, gleaming foot-high words on the wall proclaim: **"The Chamber of Secrets Has Been Opened. Enemies of the Heir, Beware."** What does it mean? In this chapter of Harry's life, he does everything that is "wizardly" possible, including risking his life to solve this 50-year-old mystery. The evil Lord Voldemort, who has been reduced to something less than human, is so feared that he is referred to only as "He-Who-Must-Not-Be-Named". This is a mockery of the Lord God! The Jews believed and some today believe that God's name, "Yahweh", meaning "I AM THAT I AM" (Exodus 3:14) was too holy to be uttered. Therefore, it is God who is to be feared and is the <u>real</u> **He-Who-Must-Not-Be-Named!**

In the folklore of the region, there is a mysterious evil presence lurking in this chamber, who has been released to roam about the school, terrorizing and killing its students as it wills. Some of the students, along with Harry's professors, suspect that Harry is the sole cause of this horrible situation, and rumors begin to fly that Harry is a practitioner of the Dark Arts. Harry is removed and cut off from the others and soon begins to wonder if he is destined to become evil.

Harry finds a secret passage into the chamber and rescues a witch girl, named Ginny, who is being held there by Voldemort. However, the Evil One was using her as bait to entrap Harry. Once he's inside the chamber, Harry fights and kills a giant serpent, called the Basilisk, then uses a fang to stab a magic diary that Voldemort uses to enchant and charm Ginny into a trance. When this diary is destroyed, the curse is lifted and Voldemort flees, beaten for the second time.

The third book in the series is entitled *Harry Potter and the Prisoner of Azkaban*. In this story, our young wizard Harry, uses his magic in an act of vengeance over something said about his mother. This causes the Dursley's dreadful visitor, Aunt Marge, to inflate like a monstrous balloon and drift up to the ceiling. Instead of being reprimanded or punished by the rest of the family, or even by his Professors who told Harry not to use his magic, he is whisked away to spend the rest of his summer in a friendly inn called "The Leaky Cauldron". It seems that Sirius Black, an escaped convict from the prison of Azkaban, is on the loose and after Harry. Sirius is another wizard (also Harry's "godfather"). He was imprisoned on the charge of murdering another wizard whom he was at odds with, named Peter Pettigrew. Once again, in this volume we have the magic of shape-shifting (the art of turning oneself into an animal), as Pettigrew faked his death and turned himself into a rat by the name of Scabbers.

A new teacher comes on the scene, one Romulus Lupus (lupus is the term for wolf); who is also a werewolf and instructor of "Defense Against the Black Arts" at Hogwart's school. The reader now becomes confused about who is good and who is evil! In the final battle, Pettigrew is turned back into human form via spells commanded by Lupus and Black. Harry wants him sent to Azkaban and not killed, as Lupus and Black intend. However, Pettigrew escapes and searches for his old "master", Voldemort.

Thus, in these books, the young reader is not only introduced to spellcasting and shape-shifting, but also to **killings** and **murders**. These are wonderful ideas to be placing into our children's minds! Don't forget, these books are specifically designed to be children's stories!

Oh yes, and if you are wondering about the cover, take a look at the creature Harry is riding. It is a mythical creature called a Griffen (half-horse, half-bird).

Once again, J.K. Rowling had children and adults alike cheering, not to mention standing in line breathlessly waiting for her next book, filled with magic and worst of all—Witchcraft!

UNDER THE SPELL OF HARRY POTTER

The "Sorcerer's Stone"

On July 8th, 2000, the fourth book of the Harry Potter series was released. It is entitled *Harry Potter and the Goblet of Fire.*

This book, unlike its predecessors, is a very thick, hardbound edition containing 734 pages and weighing approximately 2.7 pounds. At midnight on July 8th, lines at New York City's Lincoln Center Barnes & Noble bookstore stretched two city blocks, baffling late-night strollers and the surrounding store owners. In San Francisco at Cover to Cover, a tiny book and magazine shop, the staff decked themselves out in pajamas for the 400 caped and costumed children waiting to get inside the store. In Coral Gables, Florida, Books & Books threw a party with magic tricks, actors dressed as Potter characters, and a fortune-teller! In just one pre-dawn hour, they sold 200 books! At the Enchanted Forest, a small Dallas store facing off against the big chains, the owner stocked a full 600 copies, one of the highest orders ever. The books were gone within two days!

"We sold 502,000 copies online and in stores over the weekend, and 114,000 copies were sold in the first 60 minutes," marveled Mary Ellen Keating, spokesperson for Barnes & Noble, the nation's largest bookstore chain. "We're just about out of copies."

I had actually gone earlier to our local Waldenbooks store and ordered a reserved copy of the book. After all, I was still in the process of writing this book and knew that my book would be incomplete without the inclusion of a Christian view of the *Goblet of Fire* volume.

According to an article done by the *Entertainment Weekly Magazine*, dated July 1, 2000, as dawn broke in Dallas, Texas on July 8th, parties were continuing. Families lined up in the sweltering heat at 7:00 a.m., setting up impromptu tailgate parties, with coffee and breakfast. By 8:00 a.m., when the doors to the bookstore opened, local new affiliates swarmed the parking lot, and the line of people who had paid $10 to attend the two-hour party stretched to 100! When they walked in, they found the store transformed.

There were tables for magic wand-making and broomstick decorating, a corner where a sorting-hat places kids in Hogwart's houses, and a make-shift Diagon Alley (a marketplace for wizards' & witches' tools) that sold everything from robes ($29.95) to plastic slugs ($1.00). A face-painting booth provided kids with Harry's trademark lightning bolt scar!

So what about this new "wonder book"? Is it really worth the wait? Is it more innocent and fun reading? Let's take a closer look....

Before going any further, let me stop here to say that if you think that children dressing up as wizards and witches is just innocent fun, then you <u>need</u> to go back to the introduction and study the book of Deuteronomy 18:9-14! **REMEMBER, THAT ALL THESE THINGS ARE ABOMINATIONS THAT THE LORD GOD DESPISES!** If that is not enough to convince you, please consider

Exodus 22:18, which reads *"Thou shalt not suffer a witch to live."* This verse is crystal clear to me. It means: Death for Witchcraft!

Therefore, if you condone these practices, you are surely not walking in the Spirit of God! Also, if you allow your children to even remotely involve themselves in, or be representatives of these practices and abominations, then **YOU** are greatly deceived, and as the Word of God says, the truth is not in you! Harsh statement? Yes, but truth, especially God's truth, is truth, like it or not! It is we parents who have to make that choice and live by its consequences. Most important, our children also suffer the dire consequences.

So, what about *Harry Potter and the Goblet of Fire*? Has the story darkened? OH YES!

The story opens up with a murder having been committed. The police have found an entire family that, as they term it, have been "frightened to death". Of course, this in and of itself is not so shocking, (for our children to read something about murder) as they are exposed to it in some form of media nearly every day, with a constant stream of television broadcasts illustrating some form of man's inhumanity to his fellow man.

In returning to the story, the murder supposedly occurred because a local man in the town had snuck into the home of Evil Lord Voldemort, where he overheard Voldemort and his servant, Wormtail, talking and planning the murder of Harry Potter. This local, named Frank Bryce, was hiding in a secluded area of the house, until a 12-foot-long snake came up behind him, forcing Frank into the room where the two other men were plotting, and unknowingly exposing their plans to him. Voldemort becomes furious with Frank when he threatens to inform the police of their plans. After Voldemort calls Frank a "Muggle" (a term used for those who are not witches or wizards, but merely mortals), angering him, Frank then demands that the figure sitting in a wheelchair, whose face he has not been able to view, turn around and face him:

> *"Is that right?" said Frank roughly. "Lord is it?*
> *Well, I don't think much of your manners, my Lord.*
> *Turn around and face me like a man, why don't you?"* [1]

With that, Voldemort replies;

"But I am not a man, Muggle." said the cold voice, barely audible now over the crackling of the flames. "I am much more than a man. However, why not? I will face you. Wormtail, come turn my chair around." [2]

"And then the chair was facing Frank, and he saw what was sitting in it. His walking stick fell to the floor with a clatter. He opened his mouth and let out a scream. He was screaming so loudly that he never heard the words the thing in the chair spoke as it raised a wand. There was a flash of green light, and a rushing sound, and Frank Bryce crumpled. He was dead before he hit the floor." [3]

Just what killed this man? A CURSE! Referred to in the book as a killing curse, or "Avada Kedavra", a curse in which one can kill someone else in an instant, with a flash of green light! However, the penalty for a wizard using this curse is a lifetime sentence in Azkaban Prison. At the same time this murder occurs, our hero, Harry, is awakened hundreds of miles away by the lightning bolt scar on his forehead paining him. This is where the new adventure begins. Harry is spending another boring summer with his family, the Dursleys.

Harry has had a "psychic" vision of the murderous event that had just taken place. He also knew that the men sitting in the room he saw were plotting to kill someone else—namely him!

Harry also finds a book, which illustrates in detail, an odd game played on broomsticks, where each team is attempting to make a goal by putting a red ball through a 50-foot-high goal. The game is called "Quidditch". In this story, as in the others, those who hate and despise magic in any way are called "Muggles" and are viewed as being the least of God's creation! OOPS! Did I say God? Sad to say, He is **NEVER** mentioned throughout these books! The wizards are their "own" gods. They are the Masters of their own lives, not acknowledging our Father, the Creator of the Universe.

Not being able to put two and two together, Harry writes to Professor Dumbledore, to ask him about the meaning of his painful scar. He then decides to write his godfather, Sirius, who had been imprisoned in Azkaban (a terrifying jail) guarded by <u>sightless, soul-sucking fiends</u>. In the meantime, Harry's Uncle Vernon receives a letter from the parents of Ron Weasly, Harry's best friend, inviting Harry to stay with them for the summer and also to attend the Quidditch World Cup. Harry's uncle becomes enraged and can't believe they have the gall to ask for his permission to let Harry go.

It is here where we are introduced to new magical spells, such as **"Floo Powder"**, which allows the user to travel through the flues of chimneys and to "teleport" to another dimension or area through fire, without harm (much like the occult practice of projecting oneself out of their body, called astral projection). Another spell is a potion called **"Polyjuice Potion"**, that has transformative powers allowing you to masquerade as someone you know.

Are there any curses? You bet there are! We first become acquainted with the **"Imperius Curse"**, which allows you to control another's actions (a very clear goal in both Witchcraft and Satanism). With the **Cruciattus Curse**, you can inflict excruciating pain (an aspect in the practice of Voodoo, performed by sticking pins in an effigy doll of your enemy), and with the **"Avada Kedavra"** you can kill! **These words are the same as the magical expression "Abra Kedavra", used by magicians and practitioners of the Black Arts worldwide.** It is also interesting to see that in her "fantasy" writing, Rowling uses Latin words (more about that in Chapter Six).

At any rate, Harry and his friends the Weasleys transport themselves to this Quidditch World Cup Tournament, but the festivities are interrupted when Voldemort's minions, called "Death Eaters", rage across the campground with the *Dark Mark*, the sign of Voldemort. The Dark Mark is described as a "colossal skull" comprised of what looks like tiny emerald stars, along with a serpent protruding from its mouth (a very dominant symbol in the practice of Voodoo), like a tongue blazing with greenish smoke lighting up the sky.

This is the same sign Voldemort and his followers projected into the sky over the bodies of those they had <u>murdered</u> 13 years earlier. This makes everyone present extremely nervous and fearful, as they wonder if this dark denizen of evil has returned. The situation gets even more dire once Harry reaches Hogwart's. The game of Quidditch has been cancelled for the revival of the Triwizard Tournament—a perilous interschool competition. Although our hero is underage, someone illegally enters his name into the enchanted Goblet of Fire, and he is selected to compete. Harry figures out that Voldemort is up to his old tricks again. **Notice: Harry was entered into this tournament by cheating!** Even though Harry did not enter his name himself, the story now depicts: **If you want to get someplace in this life, you have to grab it by the throat and go for it, even if it means cheating to get the desired results!**

Rowling has other things in mind for our young wizard as well, such as asking a girl to the Yule Ball (changed from the word Christmas, taking the CHRIST out)! Her name is Cho Chang, and Harry has a crush on her. Prejudice also rears its ugly head, as Hagrid is excoriated publicly because his mother was a Giant, a "bloodthirsty and brutal" race of beings.

To insure that none of the students **die** during this tournament, the Ministry of Magic and the headmasters of all three of the participating schools of wizardry decide to require all competitors to be at least 17 years old, fearing that the younger wizards would not be able to avoid fatal injuries! This would have kept our hero Harry, who is only **14** years old, from putting his name into the Goblet of Fire, a magical and mystical goblet, which chooses the three student wizards who are most worthy to represent their schools. Hogwart's Headmaster, Albus Dumbledore, enforces this by encircling the goblet with a magical "age line" that can only be crossed by someone older than the age of 17. In the flame pouring forth from the goblet, the name of each student chosen for this event is revealed, and to Dumbledore's amazement, the name of Harry Potter appears!

In this game, students score points for different tasks assigned to them. The winner also receives a prize of 1,000 gold coins. The first task pits the competitors against a huge dragon, who guards a giant golden egg. Each competitor must use his/her "wizardry" skills to outwit this giant dragon and steal the egg. The second task requires each competitor to dive into the lake beside Hogwart's to rescue a friend who has been taken captive by the underwater dwellers called the "merpeople". The third task involves competitors running through a maze, which is filled with monsters, riddles, and other dangers. The outcome is that Harry and Cedric Diggory reach the Triwizard's Cup at the same time. After deciding to share in the glory, they both grab the prized object together and are suddenly transported to a graveyard!

The boys hear the words, "Avada Kedavra", at which a blast of green light hits all around them and Cedric falls dead! The next thing Harry knows, he is being bound to a marble tombstone that reads "Tom Riddle". This is Lord Voldemort's father. A helper of Voldemort then brings out a man-sized cauldron and lights a fire beneath it, bringing out of the shadows Voldemort himself, who appears to be withered and unable to walk on his own. The helper then throws the withered body into the cauldron and chants: "Bone of the father, unknowingly given, you will renew your son." [4] The helper then stretches out his own hand and using a dagger **cuts it off**! Harry watches in shock, as the blood and dismembered hand are splashed into the cauldron. (Does this sound too gory? Remember, this is what a child is reading, and these images are impressed upon his/her memory.) Not content to stop at this, Pettigrew, Voldemort's helper and assistant, walks over to our hero, and using the same dagger, slashes Harry's arm, bringing forth a surge of blood, which he catches in a vial and puts into the cauldron. This concoction then turns a brilliant white color and emits sparks into the sky. With this, the evil and vile dark Lord Voldemort arises, more powerful than ever. As other dark and evil wizards and witches materialize, they begin to pledge their allegiance to the Dark One! Voldemort, then attempts to complete what he found impossible to do 13 years earlier: **kill Harry Potter**!

All is fair in wizard war; therefore, as Voldemort gives Harry back his magic wand, he challenges him to a duel. In this part of the book,

Voldemort now tortures Harry with the Cruciatus Curse, which is outlawed, because it causes indescribable pain in the one it is used against. When Harry is hit with this curse, Rowling describes that it feels like being pierced with white-hot knives in every inch of the skin! Harry regains his composure, and this duel becomes a fight-to-the-death match, with each opponent hurling spells and curses at each other. Just then, the fatal jet of green light from Voldemort's wand, and the red light from Harry's collide in midair (sounds like *Star Wars?*), which form a golden light that fuses the two wands together and levitates both Harry and Voldemort into the air, forming a cage of light that surrounds them both. Upon a command from the spirit of Harry's deceased father, Harry breaks the connection of the lights, grabs onto his dead friend Cedric, and the two boys are magically transported back to Hogwart's school. The book ends with Headmaster Dumbledore informing the students of Cedric's death.

So, has this been another classic story of "good vs. evil" or has it been another designed story of "good" witchcraft vs. "bad" witchcraft? And what other "dark" images await the Harry Potter fan and reader? Only the next book will tell! There has been no release date for book five at the time of this writing, but it is promised to be even "darker" than its predecessors. It is to be entitled: ***Harry Potter and the Order of the Phoenix*** (a universal symbol of reincarnation).

Children are tattooed with Satanic lighting bolts.

Small children sporting the satanic lightning bolt "S" painted on their foreheads.

UNDER THE SPELL OF HARRY POTTER

Children of all ages could not wait to get their hands on *Goblet Of Fire*, as soon as it was placed on the shelves of bookstores.

Children being entertained by adult bookstore staff during a Harry Potter party, while waiting for Book Four.

CHAPTER THREE
THE WORLD OF J.K. ROWLING

I will not attempt to provide an in-depth profile on Ms. Rowling at this time, simply because if you are interested in her biography or personal profile, you will be able to find it on the web page of her publisher: http://www.Scholastic.com., and because it is not pertinent to the context of this particular book. We are more interested in where and how Ms. Rowling came up with the material for the Harry Potter books.

While literary critics have hailed her as being the catalyst for getting children away from the television and the electronic world they were so accustomed to, and back to actually reading, those same critics have failed to examine the darker side of this phenomenon.

There is no doubt that Joanne K. Rowling is a very talented storyteller who can very effectively influence and inspire children. No wonder, since she claims she grew up loving the world of the occult and was fascinated by it. Remember, this is a woman who claims she knows very little about Witchcraft and argues that she does not practice or promote it in any way! She describes her fantasy world of witches and wizards as a childhood fascination. She also describes those who inspired the characters in her books. She states that her early view of Harry was shaped by a playmate, named Ian Potter, "...whose childhood antics have startling similarities to those of the fictional schoolboy wizard."[5]

Joanne and Ian began to role-play the practices that have made her books exciting and fascinating. Ian's sister, Vikki, states:

> "We used to dress up and play witches all the time." [6]

> "My brother would dress up as a wizard. Joanne was always reading to us, and we would make secret potions for her. She would always send us off to get twigs for the potions." [7]

UNDER THE SPELL OF HARRY POTTER

As an adult, Ms. Rowling majored in Mythology at Exeter University in England. As a former wizard and Satanist myself, I can with complete assurance inform you that she has indeed, borrowed not only from the pagan rites, but has included Druidism, Witchcraft, and even Satanism in the spells, curses, and incantations used in the Harry Potter books. Ms. Rowling has clearly done extensive research on Witchcraft, otherwise it is obvious to me that we would have had witches all over the world in an uproar, claiming that the books were a misrepresentation of their craft and religion. In J. K. Rowling's world, there is only "good" magic, and the evil ones who use "bad" magic. She confuses children by differentiating the "good" from the "evil". There is no divine power of a just and loving God in her books, only witches and wizards who choose to use their "magic" for good or bad!

While many will argue that the Harry Potter books are not "real" witchcraft because the spells in the books are not legitimate spells, it is interesting to see how cleverly she uses Latin words in the incantations and curses. The principle here is that if you learn certain words, you CAN have power! The Harry Potter website is linked to a multitude of other websites on the Internet. **These websites teach you the legitimate spells and curses, and are run and maintained by actual covens of witches and Satanists!**

In an interview in *LIFE* magazine, Ms. Rowling states that she began to "receive" the idea for Harry Potter while traveling on a train and while sitting in a cafe. She began to write down the principle story line on napkins. She states:

> "The idea that we could have a child who escapes from the confines of the adult world, and go somewhere, where he has power, both literally, and metaphorically, really appealed to me." [8]

Note what she says about the child having power: that the child needs to have power and control over parents, and the power of the occult. Rowling also uses occult terms in describing her way of thinking. She says, "I have a very visual imagination. I see it, then I try to describe what is in my "mind's eye". [9] The mind's eye concept is a big part of the New Age Movement. Claiming that through it one can escape the confines of this world and explore the existence of other dimensions. Rowling remembers that she always wanted to write and that the first story she actually wrote down, when she was five or six, was a story about a rabbit called "Rabbit". Many of her favorite memories center around hearing *The Wind in the Willows*, read aloud by her father, when she had the measles. She also immensely enjoyed reading the fantastic adventure stories of E. Nesbit, reveling in the magical world of C. S. Lewis' *Chronicles of Narnia*, and her favorite story of all, *The Little White Horse* by Elizabeth Goudge.

At Exeter University, as mentioned previously, Rowling majored in Mythology and received her degree in French. She spent one year studying in Paris. After college, she moved to London to work for Amnesty International as a researcher and bilingual secretary. The best thing about working in an office, she has claimed, was typing up stories on the computer when no one was watching!

During this time, on a particularly long train ride from Manchester to London during the summer of 1990, the idea "came" to her of a boy who is a wizard and doesn't know it. She states that she could very plainly see him in her mind. By the time the train pulled into King's Cross Station four hours later, many of the characters and the early stages of the plot were fully formed in her mind. The story took further shape, as she continued working on it in pubs and cafés over her lunch hours. The book was rejected several times by publishers, until she found a London agent who sold the manuscript to Bloomsbury Children's Books. While working as a French teacher, she learned that her book about the boy wizard had been accepted for publication.

Harry Potter and the Philosopher's Stone was published in June 1997 and achieved almost instant success. With the publication of the American edition, retitled *Harry Potter and the Sorcerer's Stone* in 1998, Rowling's books continued to make publishing history. At the Bologna Book Fair, Arthur Levine, an editorial director for *Scholastic Books*, bought the American rights for $105,000, an unprecedented figure for a first-time children's author!

UNDER THE SPELL OF HARRY POTTER

In an interview published in *Books Link* magazine, Ms. Rowling, a divorced, single mother of one daughter stated, "The book is really about the power of the imagination. What Harry is learning to do is to develop his full potential. Wizardry is just an analogy I use." When asked where the ideas for the books come from, Ms. Rowling replied; "I wish I knew. Sometimes they just come [like magic?], and other times, I have to sit and think about a week, before I manage to work out how something will happen."[10]

> "Where the idea for Harry Potter actually came from, I really couldn't tell you. I was travelling on a train between Manchester and London, and it just "popped" into my head. I spent four hours, thinking about what Hogwart's would be like. It was the most interesting journey I've ever taken. By the time I got off at King's Cross, many of the characters in the books had already been invented!"[11]

When asked if there would be any more books, she replied, "Yes, even back on that train, I saw a series which would follow Harry to the end of his school days at Hogwart's (seven years). So, in the final book, Harry will have come of age in the wizardry world, and ready to leave the Dursley's at last."[12]

When reading the Harry Potter books, it becomes clear that Ms. Rowling understands MUCH more about witchcraft and wizardry than she is letting on!

Notice in this picture, sent to me by an anonymous source who testifies to being a former witch, not only is Rowling dressed in the traditional hooded witch robe, but how she also appears to be giving the witch sign, or coven greeting (arms crossed on the chest, under the chin). The photo reportedly appeared in a British magazine, edited, produced and distributed by witches for other witches, called *The Equinox*. If this source is correct, you can see how the witchcraft community praises her writings!

J.K. Rowling

THE IDEA CAME TO THE ASPIRING AUTHOR IN 1990 DURING A TRAIN RIDE FROM MANCHESTER TO LON-
don. It involved a young orphan who discovers he is a wizard, then is whisked away from his cruel
aunt and uncle to be schooled in the use of his magical powers. This year that inspiration produced
a publishing wonder: three novels about Harry Potter that keep crowding the top three spots on the
fiction best-seller lists. Movie directors with the pick of projects are jostling for the right to bring
Harry to the screen. J.K. Rowling, who lives in Edinburgh, Scotland, has four more Harry Potters
planned. Her readers, young and old, are clearing more bookshelf space now.

UNDER THE SPELL OF HARRY POTTER

Ms. Rowling has also informed her critics that she sees her books as being very "moral" and that they teach the battle between good and evil. While Ms. Rowling writes about the "good" use of occult powers and against their misuse, the "battle" lines are never defined. "Evil" is portrayed by Voldemort, who uses his powers for cruelty and control. Yet, the reader is altogether lulled into forgetting that Harry, who represents "good", uses these very **same** powers on a lesser scale!

Ms. Rowling has confused notions of authority. Magic is, and always has been, a way to bypass the authority of the Lord God, by obtaining recognition, wealth and power, by taking control of the will of others through manipulation, and tapping into the supernatural realm. Witchcraft and magic are founded upon the power of taking control, whether it is of the practitioner's life or the life of another.

In the magic world of J.K. Rowling, our children are taught to manipulate these "power" forces and reject parental authority for "self" authority. In the Harry Potter books, the witches and wizards are portrayed as the "good guys", while the parents, with their strict rules and morals, are the "bad guys"!

Rowling (the author), at home with a demonized statue.

In this photo of J.K. Rowling posing at her home, not only is she embracing a Gargoyle statue (actually an image of a demon), but also note the sun-shaped mirror behind her, flaring out. In Witchcraft, the "elements" of the universe are worshipped and harnessed, including the moon and sun.

There is NO white or black magic or witchcraft. They are the same, as they all fall under the control of the one who has authority over them—the god of this world, SATAN. The fact is, that if you practice ANY kind of magic, whether it be Witchcraft, Wizardry, or Satanism, you are under the authority of the devil!

I sincerely pray for Ms. Rowling and ask my Heavenly Father to send someone to her to introduce her to the **REAL** power, that of His Son, Jesus Christ!

On the next page are three young girls dressed in witches costumes. This is not part of a celebration of Halloween, but a Harry Potter party! Notice they are sitting in front of the witchcraft pentagram along with a Harry Potter book. Also note that they have written the magical incantation "Avada Kedavra" on the wall! These young girls have painted a circle around the pentagram and placed smaller candles around the circle, at each of the five points, with seven additional candles. It's easy to see where these young witches got this idea, as they are all wearing the round glasses of Harry, as well as the pointed hat typical of witches. Notice, too, that these young witches are also quite aware of the "horned salute" and have their fingers thrust forward with the thumbs out in the traditional witches' salutation of "SO MOTE IT BE" (translation: so shall it be). The "lead" witch in the middle is also holding the witches' altar tool of a sword in a summoning ritual.

CHAPTER FOUR
JUST WHAT IS BEING TAUGHT?

To grasp the knowledge of just how dangerous these books are in corrupting the minds of our youth, it is important and necessary to examine just what the young reader is being taught, as he/she places him/herself next to Harry in his learning experiences.

You can now spot loyal Harry Potter fans by seeing the children at Harry Potter parties across the nation, held at local bookstores and by the purple lightning bolt stickers on their foreheads. Many creative children even paint the "mark" on themselves with purple paint!

At this point, most children, as well as parents, are finding it difficult to put the books down! Once they have read them, many read them over again. They begin to closely identify with Harry and his life struggles. They also share his disappointments, as well as his fears.

They are identifying with Harry at Hogwart's as he goes through the classes on making potions, casting spells, transformations, divination, and other forms of wizardry. As they read and study how Harry learns these practices of the "old" craft, **SO DOES YOUR CHILD! This is a teaching and learning method, just as is used with Pokemon and Teletubbies.** (Read *Satan Wants Our Children,* my forthcoming book, for more in-depth information.) The fact is Satan, the oldest and most cunning of our enemies, knows that in order for him to plant his doctrines, ideologies, and belief systems into the minds of our unsuspecting children, he must present it to them, as well as their parents, as being cute, innocent, non-threatening, and exciting to participate in. This will lure them into the darkness and away from the light of God's truth! The Harry Potter book series accomplishes this agenda better than anything else on the market today.

In this magical fantasy world of Harry Potter, only two kinds of people exist. Those with powers, called wizards and witches, and those who are weak because they have NO power, despise magic, and are considered to be "normal" humans, who are referred to as Muggles!

UNDER THE SPELL OF HARRY POTTER

Being "normal" means you are not special, you are boring and mundane. But those who practice the art of forbidden occult magic are "special", and superior to normal people. And what about this fight pitting good against evil? Consider what one of Harry's Professors at Hogwart's tells him about this fight, found in *Harry Potter and the Sorcerer's Stone*: **"There is no good and evil, there is only power, and those too weak to seek it."** [13] Does this not represent "good" as being weak, and those who practice good, as being losers? God and Satan are real, and to even suggest anything else will lead someone into a world of lies! This conflict between good and evil is nothing new. It has been going on since the Lucifer-led rebellion in Heaven and continues to this very day. Therefore, Harry, our hero, is using the occult magic of divination, spells, and psychic abilities to wage this battle against the evil Lord Voldemort and his powers of darkness. Very clearly, the message here is that you fight evil with evil. You battle witchcraft with witchcraft. Let's examine some of the ideologies and beliefs being taught to our young wizard Harry:

1. Disrespect for authority. In *Harry Potter and the Sorcerer's Stone*, Harry disregards his teacher's orders and is later honored for it. Therefore, the young reader sees that breaking parental or school rules brings a reward, instead of consequences for wrongdoing. This clouds their perception of right and wrong.

2. Muggles, or humans without magic powers, are painted as being weak, and labeled "losers". To be weak and "normal" is not only boring, but unacceptable!

3. Parents and their strict rules are not to be honored. They are the "bad guys". Those with "real" power, called wizards and witches, are the "good guys".

The truth is in God's word: Ephesians 4:14-15 *"That we henceforth be no more children, tossed to and fro, and carried about with every wind of doctrine, by the sleight of men, and cunning craftiness, whereby they lie in wait to deceive; But speaking the truth in love, may grow up into him in all things, which is the head, even Christ."*

Exodus 20:12 *"Honour thy father and thy mother: that thy days may be long upon the land which the LORD thy God giveth thee."*

4. Headmaster Dumbledore tells Harry; "After all, to the well organized mind, death is but the next great adventure." [14]

Christians know that there is a glorious afterlife, but only for those who have accepted the blood atonement of the Lord Jesus Christ and have asked Him to wash them clean of their sins, through His Blood. What is being referred to here is a Witchcraft doctrine and belief. As the popular Wiccan High Priestess, known as Starhawk, states in her book, *Spiral Dance*; "Death is not an end. It is a stage in the cycle that leads to rebirth. After death, the human soul is said to rest in Summerland, the Land of Eternal Youth, where it is refreshed, grows young, and is made ready to be born again." [15]

What does the word of God say about reincarnation, and the occult version of being "born again"?

Hebrews 9:27 *"And as it is appointed unto men once to die, but after this the judgment."*

5. There is beauty in Witchcraft. Professor Snape, who teaches potions at Hogwart's states; **"I don't expect you to understand the beauty of the softly simmering cauldron, with its shimmering fumes, the delicate power of liquids, that creep through human veins, bewitching the mind, ensnaring the senses."** [16]

6. A Centaur (Greek mythological creature—half-man, half-horse) states his view on the practice of astrology: "We have sworn not to set ourselves against the heaven. Have we not read what is to come in the movement of the planets? Or have the planets not let you in on that secret?" [17] We can read in God's Word what is in store for those who look to the stars and planets for their destiny and salvation:

Isaiah 47:13-15 *"Thou art wearied in the multitude of thy counsels. Let now the astrologers, the stargazers, the monthly prognosticators, stand up, and save thee from these things that shall come upon thee. Behold, they shall be as stubble; the fire shall burn them; they shall not deliver themselves from the power of the flame: there shall not be a coal to warm at, nor fire to sit before it. Thus shall they be unto thee with whom thou hast laboured, even thy merchants, from thy youth: they shall wander every one to his quarter; none shall save thee."*

7. In all the Harry Potter books, evil is referred to as "good". The Word of God warns us about this in Isaiah 5:20-21 *"Woe unto them that call evil good, and good evil; that put darkness for light, and light for darkness; that put bitter for sweet, and sweet for bitter! Woe unto them that are wise in their own eyes, and prudent in their own sight!"*

8. Professor Quirrell, in referring to the evil and murderous wizard, Lord Voldemort states, "He is with me wherever I go. I met him when I traveled around the world. A foolish young man I was then, full of ridiculous ideas about good and evil. Lord Voldemort showed me how wrong I was. There is no good and evil, there is only power, and those too weak to seek it. Since then, I have served him faithfully." [18]

How utterly ridiculous this statement is! He is saying that it took a wizard practicing black magic to show him the "truth" behind the concept of good and evil. To say there is no evil, is calling God Himself a LIAR— a very dangerous thing to do! Therefore, according to Harry Potter, Satan is not evil, but good, because he has "powers" and knows how to use them! R-i-i-i-ght!

9. Hagrid, the grounds-keeper at Hogwart's, tells Harry about the strange power that saved his life; "Happened when a powerful, evil curse touches you. Didn't work on you [Harry], and that's why yer famous Harry. No one ever lived after he (Voldemort) decided to kill 'em, no one except you." [19]

Notice how Harry appears to be almost Christlike, with his mark or wound, his psychic powers, and his victory over death itself! Also in this story, we have to wonder just why Ms. Rowling chose to call her convict character "Sirius". After all, Sirius was a powerful Egyptian god who appeared to man as part-man, part-cat. They even named a star after this god, in his honor, giving him special place in the stellar kingdom for Pharos, known as Orion. Also, in this third installment, the reader is introduced to spiritism, palmistry, astrology, shape-shifting, and even time travel. No wonder our youth crave more. Very few children have the biblical knowledge and discernment needed to evaluate good and evil or to resist these threats to their faith. Azkaban is an isolated prison-fortress for criminal wizards. Ah, seems not all is "perfect" in this wizard wonderland! The guards there are called "Dementors", and are terrifying "Grim Reaper" style creatures, who can literally "suck" the happiness out of someone.

10. Witchcraft is to be fought with Witchcraft. In *Harry Potter and the Sorcerer's Stone*, it is revealed that both the magic wand of Harry and the wand of the evil Voldemort contain a Phoenix feather, which is its power source. It is clear then, that both Harry, representing the "good" wizard, and Voldemort, representing the "evil" wizard, are using the same source of power. Their Witchcraft is one and the same!

11. Rebellion against parental and adult authority. In Hogwart's, we find a school that has an organized system of rules, much like any other school. However, Harry's disobedience, as he frequently breaks these rules is pretty much overlooked, and our young wizard is even rewarded by the authority figures in this school. Harry even blackmails his uncle and uses trickery, lies, and deception in breaking the rules! At one point, when an aunt says something derogatory about Harry's mother, Harry uses a spell, which inflates this aunt like a balloon and sends her sailing upwards towards the ceiling. Harry did this even though he was instructed NOT to flaunt or use his magic outside of Hogwart's, and only with strict supervision. Again, instead of being reprimanded, he is rewarded. Harry frequently tells lies to get himself out of trouble, and lets his fellow students provoke him into revenge.

In one of the books, Hermione, the female friend of Harry, wants to join in and "buddy" with Harry and his friend Ron, but is not accepted. A situation arises in which the truth could bring punishment to both Harry and Ron. This results in Hermione lying for them and is immediately rewarded by being accepted into the "fold". Harry "hates" his enemies, and the young reader is soon forgiving of Harry, seeing that those against him **deserve** what they get! Ms. Rowling does a good job of defining those who are "weak" and despise magic as not only being Muggles, but losers, fat, and worthless e.g., the Dursley's.

In the Harry Potter books, we find NO good role models. In fact, those who do obey authority are looked upon as being "weak" and "hypocritical". Below are some clear examples of this:

> **"That, said Ron fervently, was the best story you've ever come up with [showing praise for telling lies]."[20]**

> **"Mum, shut up! Ron yelled...."[21]**

> **"I never thought I'd see the day when you'd [Hermione] be persuading us to break rules," said Ron. "Alright, we'll do it."[22]**

> **"I will not be spoken to like that!" said Uncle Vernon, trembling with rage. But Harry wasn't going to stand for this. Gone were the days when he had been forced to take every single one of the Dursley's stupid rules."[23]**

> **Finally, Harry continues to tell lies...[24]**

Ms. Rowling introduces the concept of sin in a deceptive manner. Her concept of sin is introduced through a "good" witch in her books filled with blood drinking, sacrifices, divination, spellcasting, hexes and curses, and other forms of occult practices; teaching the young reader that those who practice these things are NOT rebellious or sinners, even in the eyes of the Lord Almighty, unless they use these powers for blind ambition. Harry lies, cheats, hates people, breaks rules, despises authority, and plots; but the way his actions are presented in the Potter books appears to make these things acceptable! Ms. Rowling is right when she states that she feels these books are very moral; the problem is that her view of morality directly contradicts the Word of God's definition of morality!

Let's take a look at how the parental characters in the Potter books are portrayed:

> **Mr. Weasley was insisting on taking the Grangers off to the Leaky Cauldron for a drink. [25]**

> **"Thought I wouldn't say no to a large bottle of Ogden's Old Firewhiskey!" [26]**

> **Percy heaved an impressive sigh and took a deep swig of elderflower wine... [27]**

> **"She's gone," said Hermione. "Why don't we go and have a butterbeer in the Thee Broomsticks [a pub]?" [28]**

> **The pub was crowded as ever. He [Harry] went up to the bar with Ron and Hermione, ordered three butterbeers.... [29]**

It seems our young characters are not only into witchcraft, but drinking and gambling as well! [30]

12. Revenge and hatred towards enemies.

> **"It's not possible to live with the Dursleys, and not hate them," said Harry. [31]**

"I wouldn't mind knowing how Riddle got awarded for special services to Hogwart's either. Could've been anything," said Ron. "Maybe he murdered Myrtle, that would've done everyone a favor." [32]

"I hate that Skeeter woman," she [Hermione] bursts out savagely. [33]

The Lord Jesus Christ taught and instructed otherwise: Matthew 5:44 *"But I say unto you, Love your enemies, bless them that curse you, do good to them that hate you, and pray for them which despitefully use you, and persecute you."*

ULTIMATELY, OUR CHILDREN ARE LEARNING "REAL" WITCHCRAFT! When asked in an interview how Ms. Rowling felt about Fundamental Christians, she replied: **"I think they need psychiatric help. I say, honestly, can they read some of them [books]? I think they [books] are moral. By and large, they [book characters] go with their conscience, which is a powerful thing. There you go." [34]**

Rowling also states: **"I decided on the school subjects very early on. Most of the spells are invented, but some of them have a basis in what people used to believe worked. We owe a lot of our scientific knowledge to alchemists!" [35]**

Ah, Ms. Rowling, what a statement you have made! You state that "most" of the spells are invented, BUT that some of them are actual "witchcraft" spells! It is also funny how Ms. Rowling uses Latin words in many of the "curses" found in the books.

The faithful pet Phoenix of our young wizard is named "Fawkes". Could it be that Ms. Rowling is using this name to refer to the actual man, Guy Fawkes, about whom history books tell us that he **attempted to blow up the English Parliament in order to stop the King James**

Bible from being translated and printed? In an interview, when asked about how Ms. Rowling felt about Halloween and Guy Fawkes Day, she replied, **"That's unusual that you know about that. You got the joke about Fawkes, the Phoenix."** [36]

I had heard, from a very reliable source, that Warner Brothers had planned on a premiere showing of the *Harry Potter and the Sorcerer's Stone* movie at a major London theatre on November 5th. I then decided to do some research on Guy Fawkes Day, and guess what? It, too, is celebrated on November 5th! From the information that I gathered, I discovered that this plot to keep the King James Bible from being translated and printed was foiled during the night between the 4th and 5th of November, 1605. Already on November 5th, agitated Londoners, who knew little more than that their King had been saved, joyfully lit bonfires in thanksgiving. As years progressed, however, the ritual became more elaborate.

Soon people began placing effigies onto bonfires, and fireworks were added to the celebrations. Effigies of Guy Fawkes, and sometimes those of the Pope, graced these fires. Still today, some communities throw dummies of both Guy Fawkes and the Pope onto the bonfire. On the night itself, the Guy Fawkes effigy is placed on top of the bonfire, which is then set on flames, and firework displays fill the sky. The ceremony of the burning is much the same as the fires in which those accused of Witchcraft were burned alive!

Could it be just a fascinating coincidence that the release date of the new movie was scheduled to premiere on this night?

Let's examine one prime example of a child immersing herself in the Harry Potter books. In Lock Haven, Pennsylvania, lives a little girl names Ashley Daniels. She is as close as you can get to your typical nine-year-old American girl. A third grader at Lock Haven Elementary School, she loves rollerblading, her pet hamsters Benny and Oreo, Britney Spears, and of course, Harry Potter. Having breezed through the most recent Potter opus in just four days, Ashley is among the millions of children who have made *Harry Potter and the Goblet of Fire* the fastest-selling book in publishing history. And, like many of her school friends, Ashley was captivated enough by the strange occult doings at the Hogwart's School of Witchcraft and Wizardry to pursue the Left-Hand Path, determined to become as adept at the black arts as Harry and his pals.

A newsletter article reports: **"I used to believe in what they taught us at Sunday School,"** said Ashley, conjuring up an ancient spell to summon Cerebus, the three-headed hound of hell in the Potter series, **"But, the Harry Potter books showed me that magic is real, something I can use right now, and that the Bible is nothing but boring lies!"** [37]

Parents, did you hear the DANGER in that statement? Harry Potter has made the magic of witchcraft and sorcery exciting, but the Bible—boring! Is this what the Harry Potter books are designed to do? The devil has definitely found a very effective tool to bring into the home and destroy the family unit. Children of all ages are now doing what Harry Potter does, emulating who he is, and believing what he believes. Harry is a powerful young wizard with a long history of generational witchcraft! This is why there are Harry Potter parties, with children dressed as their favorite "witch" characters, including the lightning bolt mark painted on their foreheads; armed with paraphernalia that teaches them to cast spells and curses, read crystal balls and Tarot cards, and pretend to turn themselves into animals! Yet, most parents, even some Christian parents, see **nothing** wrong with these books! **GOD HELP US.**

Listen to what High Priest Egan of the First Church of Satan in Salem, Massachusetts has to say about the Potter books: **"Harry is an absolute godsend to our cause. An organization like ours, thrives on "new blood", no pun intended, and, we've had more applicants than we can handle lately."** [38] Here, we actually have SATANISTS praising the Harry Potter books. What's wrong with this picture?

There is power in spellcasting. Throughout the Harry Potter books, witches and wizards are conjuring up all kinds of spells, hexes, and curses to get revenge on an enemy or play tricks on others. At Hogwart's, students casting spells on other students had gotten so out of hand that the administration issued a proclamation forbidding any more of this. Throughout the Potter books, spells are not easily reversed, and anti-spells or potions are concocted just to reverse or cancel a curse or spell that has been placed over another. Clearly, the message to the young reader is **"Fight Witchcraft with Witchcraft!"**

On the campus of Hogwart's, we find the following four fraternity houses—three are for "White" Magic and one for "Black" Magic:

1. *SLYTHERIN*- Described as "the house that turned out more Dark witches and wizards than any other." **"Being able to talk to snakes was what Salazar Slytherin was famous for. That's why the symbol of Slytherin, is a serpent."** [39] In this house, the evil fraternity members have green eyes that match the serpent symbol. It is interesting to note here that Harry also has green eyes. However, since he didn't make the choice to follow the path of the Dark side, he is NOT evil!

2. *GRYFFINDOR*- Described as a White Magic Fraternity House where Harry was sent by the magical Sorting Hat. **It is significant that Harry was almost sent to the Slytherin house by the Sorting Hat because the hat could sense the Dark Magic characteristics in our young wizard!** Harry is sent to Gryffindor after complaining about being sent to Slytherin.

3. *HUFFLEPUFF & RAVENCLAW*- Both houses of White Magic

At Hogwart's, the Herbology class is taught by a Professor Sprout who teaches about plants. However, these are no **ordinary** plants! The plants used in the class are found only in this fantasy world. They are used to make potions and anti-potions for the witches to use in their spell-casting.

The Mandrake is an actual plant and is shaped like a man. During the time that I was actually studying witchcraft in Oklahoma, we used these plants. Legend has it that these plants are found in the ground, near a tree where there had been a hanging. As the semen of the victim fell upon the ground, the plant took root. This is why it is shaped like a man. It is a powerful drug; when broken down, boiled, and used in a potion form, it can have a strong aphrodisiac effect or can bring the will of a person under the control of another. It must be pulled out by all of the roots and is said let out a "cry" when removed from the ground. This is the very same plant referred to in *Harry Potter and the Chamber of Secrets*!

Professor Sprout was standing behind a thestle bench in the center of the greenhouse. About twenty pairs of different-colored earmuffs were lying on the bench. When Harry had taken his place between Ron and Hermione, she [Sprout] said; "We'll be repotting Mandrakes today. Now, who can tell me the properties of the Mandrake?" To nobody's surprise, Hermione's hand was first into the air. "Mandrake, or Mandragora, is a powerful restorative," said Hermione, sounding as usual, as though she had swallowed the textbook. "It is used to return people who have been transfigured or cursed, back to their original state."

"Excellent. Ten points for Gryffindor," said Professor Sprout. "The Mandrake forms an essential part of most antidotes. It is also, however, dangerous. Who can tell me why?" Once again, Hermione's hand was first to be raised, as she explained that the cry of the Mandrake is fatal to anyone who hears it.

She [Sprout] pointed to a row of deep trays as she spoke, and everyone shuffled forward for a better look. A hundred or so tufty little plants, purplish in color, were growing there in rows. They looked quite remarkable to Harry, who didn't have the slightest idea what Hermione meant by the "cry" of the Mandrake.

Sprout then tells the students to put the earmuffs on securely, and that she will give the sign when it is okay to remove them.

> **Harry let out a gasp of surprise that no one could hear. Instead of roots, a small, muddy, and extremely ugly baby popped out of the earth. The leaves were growing right out of his head. He had pale green, mottled skin, and was clearly bawling at the top of his lungs. [40]**

Note that Rowling employs a real plant used in witchcraft in the story and writes a human baby into the story line, who forms the root system of the plant!

> **Then, Professor Sprout told the class; "As our Mandrakes are only seedlings, their cries won't kill yet. However, they will knock you out for several hours." [41]**

Imagine, if you will, your child reading this story. What kind of things are going through the mind of that child as this story unfolds? I have to agree with Ms. Rowling when she makes the statement that the ideas for these things "popped" into her head. My question is, "Who, or what put them there?" She seems to have gained a vast knowledge of the occult at this point in her writing of the Harry Potter saga! Can you imagine the psychological shock and trauma this picture would have on a young child?

While these are not presented as being "human" babies, one can't help but think about the argument given by abortion rights activists who say that the baby forming in the mother's womb is not really human, but merely "tissue" labeled as "a fetus". These are definitely NOT the types of things the scripture tells us to think about. Paul tells us:

Philippians 4:8 *"Finally, brethren, whatsoever things are true, whatsoever things are honest, whatsoever things are just, whatsoever things are pure, whatsoever things are lovely, whatsoever things are of good report; if there be any virtue, and if there be any praise, think on these things."*

UNDER THE SPELL OF HARRY POTTER

Do you get the "gist" of what is being portrayed here? Young children are being murdered in order to make witch potions. This is reality: these atrocities are going on even to this day!

There is definitely a "Pied Piper" who is steering our children away from the parental authority of the home, as well as away from God's laws, and leading them toward the path of destruction through Witchcraft, Satanism, and other devices of Satan's kingdom. His name is Harry Potter!

Is the Alchemy and Sorcery in Harry Potter real? In order to answer that question, we need to have an understanding of what alchemy is. In *Harry Potter and the Sorcerer's Stone*, alchemy is central to the plot of the story. Remember, this title was originally *Harry Potter and the Philosopher's Stone*. The philosopher's stone is connected to alchemy, which is an occult practice that combined the exploration of minerals with Gnostic practices of sorcery. The goal was to turn base metal into gold, and through that attaining an inner spiritual transformation. Rowling refers to Nicolas Flamel, a character in *Harry Potter and the Sorcerer's Stone*, as the partner of Albus Dumbledore performing alchemy. Harry and his friends search through the library to see just who this Nicolas Flamel is. They finally discover that he is the "only maker of the Sorcerer's Stone" which has the ability to turn metal into gold, and also gives immortality through producing the "Elixir of Life". In the book, Flamel has achieved this immortality, because we are told he is 665 years old! Flamel is also mentioned several times in the book *Witchcraft, Magic & Alchemy*, by Grillot de Givry.

Rowling describes Flamel and his wife, named Perenelle, as being over 600 years old. In Spence's *Encyclopedia of Occultism*, the name of Flamel's wife's is Petronella. Flamel first studied astrology before coming across a book with instructions and pictures of serpents, which was purported to be a magical book written by a magician named Abraham. This led Flamel to further studies and he is reported as achieving the ability to turn mercury into gold, as well as discovering the "Elixir of Life". So if Flamel and Dumbledore were partners, then this makes Dumbledore, Harry's favorite instructor and Headmaster of Hogwart's, a practitioner of the occult!

OTHER FORMS OF THE OCCULT
FOUND IN HARRY POTTER:

MUGGLES - Non-witches and wizards are referred to as "Muggles". In the Italian language, muggle is translated as "Babbani", meaning idiots!

GHOSTS - We find ghosts throughout the *Harry Potter and the Sorcerer's Stone*, as each of the four fraternity houses has a resident ghost in them. Harry is also able to see his deceased parents by looking into a magical mirror, allowing him to communicate with them.

We are forbidden to even attempt to contact the spirits of the dead in God's word (Leviticus 19:31, 20:6; Deuteronomy 18:10-11 and Isaiah 8:19). This mirror is also used for divination (foretelling future events). Children are often confused about the concept of ghosts and whether the spirits of our departed actually roam the earth in spirit-form, thus it appears that the Harry Potter books not only encourage them to make contact with these spirits, but that it is also a "good" thing to do.

DIVINATION - The magical mirror that Harry uses to see his dead parents is called the "Mirror of Erised", which is the word "desire" spelled backward. When our young wizard looks into the mirror to get a vision that will give him the location of the Sorcerer's Stone, the stone actually manifests and materializes in Harry's pocket. [42] In the occult practice of divination, mirrors, crystal balls, ouija boards, tarot cards, and even cauldrons of water are used to see things which have been hidden from "normal" eyes. The magic mirror is a favorite tool of divination for the witch. (See, even the story of *Snow White and the Seven Dwarfs*, had witchcraft components in it!)

This practice is referred to as "Scrying", in which the reflective face of a mirror is painted black, and as the practitioner concentrates and gazes into the face, it is said they will see a vision of what they are desiring to see.

THE MAGIC WAND - Harry is taken to Diagon Alley, a marketplace of wizardry and witchcraft tools, to choose a magic wand. Many wands pass through his hands, but he is told that it is the wand that chooses the wizard rather than the wizard choosing the wand! **Wands** are also known in the occult as "divining rods" used for purifying, divination, focusing energy into a spell, finding water or even treasure, and invoking spirits. In the occult, it is often believed that Moses was a great magician who triumphed over the Egyptians and parted the Red Sea through sorcery with his staff.

The truth is, it was God himself who performed these miracles, using Moses (Exodus 4:6-11, 14:21).

SPIRIT COMMUNICATION - In *Harry Potter and the Sorcerer's Stone*, Harry visits the zoo, where he discovers he is able to communicate with snakes! In fact, this snake is a boa constrictor, which is able to magically escape from its cage after a telepathic communication between the two. In the occult, serpents have a special place. They are symbols of fertility, wisdom, and enlightenment. It is also the symbol used to represent the devil, Satan, and is found in the book of Genesis, tempting Eve in the Garden of Eden. It is significant that Harry is able to communicate with a serpent. Oh yes, Voldemort also has the ability to communicate with serpents, and he is also symbolized as a "serpent" being!

MIND READING - At Hogwart's, a magical tool, called a Sorting Hat, is used to determine which of the four houses a student should be placed. The hat itself makes this decision and is also able to read the mind of the student, giving it the knowledge level of the student and aiding it in making that decision. In the real world, there are seminars held worldwide which offer training in the development of an individual's power to read minds, tap into his/her psychic powers, and develop skills in mental telepathy.

THE CASTING OF SPELLS AND CURSES - Throughout the Harry Potter books, spells, hexes, and curses are frequently used, as well as taught, at Hogwart's. Harry even uses a "body-binding" spell on one of his friends. The book, *A Witches' Bible*, contains specific instructions on how to perform a spell for binding! [43]

In the books, spells and the interest in spells are promoted and portrayed as being good things. For example, when the students are on the train going to Hogwart's, Ron is asked to perform a spell. When he can't do it, Hermione steps in and states that she has already performed a number of "simple" spells and had success with them.

Today, spell-casting books are easily found in all kinds of bookstores. In addition, the Internet is FULL of websites where one can go and actually receive instruction for casting spells, hexes, and curses from an actual practitioner of the occult arts! Many teenagers are flocking to these sites, searching for a way to become more attractive to the opposite sex, gain fame and fortune, and even how to place spells on teachers to receive good grades in school.

During my multi-city tour for The Prophecy Club®, who allowed me to speak out about Harry Potter, Pokemon, Teletubbies, Furbies, video games, and other devices being used to lure our youth into Witchcraft and Satanism, I identified one of the most popular witches with the teenagers, Silver Ravenwolf, whose book *Teen Witch*, is a best-seller in bookstores. She gives the disillusioned and often neglected teenager hope of becoming popular, appreciated, and able to succeed in the world by becoming a witch and practicing the "craft"! The book is filled with instructions for different rituals and spells for the teen to perform in order to achieve these goals. One only needs to read Deuteronomy 18 to see whether these devices actually work or not. **THE LORD GOD STRICTLY FORBIDS THEIR USE!**

BLACK MAGIC BLOOD RITUALS - In Satanism and the "darker" practices of the occult, blood sacrifices and the drinking of blood is always prevalent. One sees it in stories about vampires, and it occurs during real Black Masses held by Satanists.

Occultists have known that there is "life" power in blood for centuries! After all, it is the Blood of Jesus Christ shed as He died on the cross at Calvary that has the power to cleanse us from sin. It is also His Blood that gives us power over the demons! Hallelujah! It is the power of His Blood that sets us free. Witches and Satanists do not see the act of the sacrifice itself as the source of releasing power, but the shedding of the blood of the victim. They believe it has a life-giving power and that they can tap into this energy by the letting and drinking of blood.

In *Harry Potter and the Sorcerer's Stone*, the Dark Lord Voldemort drinks the blood of a unicorn to gain power. In *Harry Potter and the Goblet of Fire*, Voldemort launches an elaborate plan to ensnare Harry through instructing his servant, Pettigrew, to take some of Harry's blood and make a potion, which will restore Voldemort to his former state of power. A graphic description of this ritual is contained in Chapter Two.

SEXUAL MAGIC - Sexual magic is very important to the witch. It gives the witch her energy and is often used in rituals and spellcasting. It is also used to gain control over another. In *Harry Potter and the Goblet of Fire*, the spice of sexuality is added as Harry begins to mature, and reference is made to "private parts". In addition, students are described as pairing off and "going into the bushes".

BLACK MAGIC - In the Harry Potter books, references are made to the evil Voldemort ("mort" being French for "death" ...remember Rowling was a French teacher) and others having gone over to the "dark side" (shades of the "Dark Force" in Star Wars). What is implied here is that people are not inherently bad, but either basically good or morally neutral and can go either way. This down-plays evil itself and distorts the idea of good and evil. The occult philosophy denies any conflict between good and evil. In the *Harry Potter and the Sorcerer's Stone*, Professor Quirell, who serves Voldemort, can't touch our young wizard because Harry was so deeply loved and protected by his mother (a witch herself). This characterization implies that human love can ward off evil.

With this philosophy, there is no need for redemption or salvation, as one is able to produce their own. As Anton Szandor LaVey, founder and former High Priest of the First Church of Satan, wrote in his book, *The Satanic Bible*; **"Look to thyself and say, I am mine own redeemer."** [44] This is a strong concept in Satanism. There is NO need for a Savior, as you become your own! Voldemort, who is described as being **"not truly alive (so) he cannot be killed."** [45] (He is his own lifegiver.)

WHITE MAGIC - There is a popular claim made by witches today that they do not serve evil, as they use their magic for "good". This concept is prevalent in the Harry Potter books, as Harry and his friends are learning to use their magic in a good way. In fact, the "good" wizards in the story use sorcery to combat the "dark" forces. At the same time, they are studying how to cast spells and protect themselves through charms, potions, etc.

The Word of God makes it very clear in Deuteronomy 18 that if you are practicing **ANY** form of witchcraft, whether you call it "good", "bad", "white" or "black", **IT IS AN ABOMINATION [the greatest of sins in God's eyes]. If the practitioner does not turn from it and receive salvation offered through Jesus Christ, the penalty for such practices is DEATH!** There is no white or grey witchcraft—it all comes from the Satanic domain!

REBELLION - Harry is constantly in rebellion and defiance of authority. This is a MUST, if you are to be a witch! He even uses magic in revenge, to get back at his cousin, Dudley: **"They don't know we're not allowed to use it [magic] at home. I'm going to have a lot of fun with Dudley this summer."** [46] This is also how the first book ends, with our hero exhibiting rebellion and revenge!

After the death of Flamel and his wife, when the Sorcerer's Stone is destroyed, Dumbledore remarks: **"Truth is a beautiful and terrible thing, and should therefore be treated with great caution."** [47] So, if truth is such a terrible thing, then is it better to be in rebellion by telling lies?

SPIRIT POSSESSION - In one of the Harry Potter books, Voldemort "possesses" the body of one of Harry's professors to get near Harry. In *Harry Potter and the Chamber of Secrets*, Harry must rescue a little girl who has been possessed by Voldemort and made to commit murder!

It is clear that even though the Harry Potter books are portrayed as "fantasy", the element of truth and realism of witchcraft practiced by those who are "real" witches is also interwoven into the stories. In conclusion, I want you to contemplate the following facts and ultimate question. There has been much said about how Ms. Rowling wrote the early Harry Potter stories on scraps of paper, while on a train and in a café, and while unemployed. She claims that the books spring unaided from her imagination. However, the fact stands that **Ms. Rowling did NOT imagine the practices of astrology, blood sacrifices, casting spells, witchcraft, placing of curses on others, alchemy, charms, scrying, magic wands, white and black magic, Nicolas Flamel, as well as all other occult information the books contain! Once again, these things did NOT come from the imagination of one J.K. Rowling. It appears that Ms. Rowling herself, has a vast knowledge of these practices**.

It is also easy to see that Harry Potter glorifies the occult. The occult is severely condemned by the Lord God. Then should we take such books so lightly? Should we, as parents, accept them as being perfectly all right for our children to read under the guise of being merely "fantasy"?

CHAPTER FIVE
WHAT THEY ARE SAYING
ABOUT HARRY

*I*t seems that people practically everywhere are singing the praises of the Harry Potter books. Everyone—from educators, children, parents, and sadly, even popular, prominent Christian leaders—is heralding these books on witchcraft and wizardry as being moral, and great tools "to get our children reading again." Even the author herself gives praise to Harry Potter and denies any danger inherent in this "fantasy" witchcraft. In an interview with *Newsweek* magazine's Malcom Jones, she observed, **"I get letters from children addressed to Professor Dumbledore, and it's not a joke, begging to be let into Hogwart's, and some of them are really sad, because they want it to be true so badly, they've convinced themselves it's true."** [48]

In a recent report published in *Christianity Today*, it was clear to see that the magazine based its approval of the Harry Potter books NOT on the Bible, but on the popular consensus among the admired Christian leaders who were okaying it. Ted Olsen, the author of the report, wrote:

> **"As far as I can tell, while no major Christian leader has come out to condemn J.K. Rowling's series, many have given it the thumbs-up. If our readers know of any major Christian leader who has actually told Christians not to read the books, I'd be happy to know about it; but, in my research, even those Christians known for criticizing all that is popular culture, have been pretty positive about Potter."** [49]

To prove his point, Mr. Olsen quoted from seven "Christian" leaders and publications:

UNDER THE SPELL OF HARRY POTTER

Chuck Colson, during his _Breakpoint_ radio broadcast on November 2, 1999, commended Harry and his friends for their "courage, loyalty, and a willingness to sacrifice for one another, even at the risk of their own lives. The Witchcraft practices in the book are purely mechanical, as opposed to the occult. That is, Harry, and his friends, cast spells, read crystal balls, and turn themselves into animals, but they don't make contact with a supernatural world. It's not the kind of real-life Witchcraft the Bible condemns." [50]

It is apparent to me, that either Mr. Colson NEVER read a Harry Potter book, he is working for the "other" side, or he is gravely deceived. There is no other explanation for him making such ridiculous statements. Witchcraft is Witchcraft—regardless of WHAT form it takes! If Mr. Colson would spend more time in God's Word and less time in the Harry Potter books, he would find that in Deuteronomy 18, God Himself sees NO difference between so-called "mechanical witchcraft" and the REAL thing!

Dr. James Dobson, founder of the popular _Focus On The Family_, an organization designed to promote better Christian living, also endorsed the Harry Potter books by stating that they were merely "fantasy" witchcraft! [51]

World Magazine also praised _Harry Potter and the Sorcerer's Stone_, as **"a delight, with a surprising bit of depth."** In fact, the article's author, Roy Maynard, assured the magazine's readers that:

> **"Rowling keeps it safe, inoffensive, and non-occult. This is the realm of Gandalf, and the wizard of Id, not Witchcraft. There is a fairy-tale order to it all, in which, as Chesterton, and Tolkien pointed out, magic must have rules, and good, does not, cannot, mix with bad."** [52]

This same magazine, in another issue, contained a second article, which toned down the first one stating:

> **"A reader drawn in, would find that the real world**

of Witchcraft, is not Harry Potter's world. Neither attractive, nor harmless, it is powerful, and evil." [53]

The *British Christianity* magazine praised the series. In one of its issues, Mark Greene, Director of the London Institute For Contemporary Christianity, wrote a note describing his regrets over not giving the Harry Potter book to his goddaughter earlier by stating:

> **"I wish I'd been the one to introduce her to Harry. Fine lad you know, courageous, resourceful, humble, fun, good mind. Comes from good stock, you know. She could do worse, far worse. And, as far as literary companions go, frankly, not much better." [54]**

An editorial in *Christian Century*, entitled "Wizards and Muggles," stated:

> **"Rowling is not the first fantasy writer to be attacked by conservative Christians. Even the explicitly Christian writer, Madeleine L'Engle, has taken heat for the magic elements in *A Wrinkle In Time*. Such critics are right in thinking that fantasy writing is powerful and needs to be taken seriously. But, we strongly doubt that it fosters an attachment to evil powers. Harry's world, in any case, is a moral one." [55]**

Focus On The Family gave a mixed review. As Ted Olsen wrote in his report, Focus' critic, Lindy Beam, simply observed;

> **"Apart from the benefit of wise adult guidance in reading these books, it is best to leave Harry Potter on the shelf." [56]**

Alan Jacobs, Professor at Wheaton College, states that the Harry Potter stories promote:

> **"...a kind of spiritual warfare... a struggle between good and evil. There is, in books like this, the possibility for serious moral reflection... the question of what to do with magic powers, is explored in an appropriate and morally serious way."** [57]

Doesn't it state in God's Word that if it were possible, even the very elect (those in the know) would be deceived? This prophecy has surely been fulfilled!

The fact is, whether one calls it "mechanical", "fantasy witchcraft", or "white and black magic", they are all an **ABOMINATION TO GOD**, and **NONE** of them are **GOOD!**

Isaiah 5:20-21 bears repeating: *"Woe unto them that call evil good, and good evil; that put darkness for light, and light for darkness; that put bitter for sweet, and sweet for bitter! Woe unto them that are wise in their own eyes, and prudent in their own sight!"*

John Monk, an editorial writer for *The State In Columbia*, says;

> **"Though set mostly in a wizard's world, the Potter books promote, through their characters, friendship, love, bravery, self-reliance, the importance of family and tolerance toward those different from us. They depict the quest for knowledge, wisdom, and right action, the universal journey every human takes."** [58]

The characters in the Harry Potter books also lie, steal, cheat, rebel, and seek revenge!

The idea of using Witchcraft to fight Witchcraft is a major component of the story lines in the Harry Potter book series. In a 1996 movie entitled, *The Craft*, audiences watched as a group of four teenage girls (who were witches) have fun while practicing spell-casting; when suddenly, a spirit-invoking ritual backfired on them. This resulted in the group leader becoming demon possessed and turned two other members of the group to the "dark" side. The one remaining girl, who wasn't turned to the dark side, desperately tries to remain a "good" white witch, but the other three continually attempt to destroy her. Fearing she will bring harm to the group, the "white" witch allows herself to be possessed in order to use spells to combat the others. The movie concludes with the group leader institutionalized in a mental hospital, as a result of a "binding" spell. This leaves the other two girls with a new leader (the once "white" witch) and they're not sure whether to befriend her or not. The initially "good" witch then calls down supernatural powers, causing a bolt of lightning to strike and break off a large tree branch, barely missing the other two girls, letting them know she is still the one most powerful. This movie helped to promote teenage witchcraft and attracted many teenage girls to Wicca.

In June of 1999, Silver Ravenwolf's *Teen Witch* had sold more than 50,000 copies! It is this same concept that sells the Harry Potter books.

Below are what REAL witches are saying about Harry Potter:

In an interview with *Newsweek* magazine, a spokesperson for the Pagan Federation in England, when asked his opinion of the Harry Potter phenomenon stated;

> **"Naturally, the island's Pagan Federation is pleased. Though it refuses to admit new members under the age of 18, it deals with an average of 100 inquiries a month, from youngsters who want to become witches, and has occasionally been swamped with calls."** [59]

This organization also issued a statement saying;

> **"The Pagan Federation has appointed a youth officer, to deal with a flood of inquiries, following the success of the Harry Potter books, which describe magic and wizardry."** [60]

UNDER THE SPELL OF HARRY POTTER

An article in the December 17th, 2000 issue of *Time* magazine, reported that a similar organization in Germany was also dealing with an increasing number of inquiries from youngsters of all ages. Worldwide librarians are reporting that children, in increasing numbers, are requesting materials from the occult sections. Many of the occult books are also being stolen from these libraries—for their content!

Finally, read what the Satanists, themselves, are saying about Harry Potter:

As a former Satanist myself, I frequently use the Internet to tap into specific satanic websites to see what they are doing and saying. In order to thwart his plans, I believe we **must** know our enemy and how he operates—a universal military strategy. With the popularity of the Harry Potter book series, I was sure one of the satanic sites would have some sort of remarks about them, and I was right! One of these particular websites had an article on Harry Potter stating:

> **"In 1995, it was estimated that some 100,000 Americans, mostly adults, were involved in devil-worship groups. Today, more than 14 million children alone, belong to the Church Of Satan, thanks largely to the unassuming boy wizard from 4 Privet Drive (Harry's street address)."** [61]

Imagine, Harry Potter books being praised by Satanists as a great recruiting tool! This article included comments from young Satanists. One of the comments came from 6 year-old Jessica Lehman of Easley, South Carolina stating:

> **"Hermione is my favorite, because she's smart and has a kitty. Jesus died, because he was weak, and stupid."** [62]

Can you feel the hatred towards Christianity in this comment? Keep in mind, their goal is wipe Christianity and any trace of God off the earth!

WHAT THEY ARE SAYING ABOUT HARRY

Another comment comes from 11 year-old Bradley Winters, who stated:

> **"The Harry Potter books are awesome! When I grow up, I'm going to learn Necromancy, and summon greater demons to Earth."** [63]

Take note: Through the Harry Potter book series, this young boy implies that he has been introduced to Necromancy (summoning demons and spirits of the dead), a practice totally condemned in God's Word.

The author of this satanic article concluded the article with the following statement:

> **"I think it's absolute rubbish, to protest children's books, on the grounds that they are luring children to Satan. People should be praising them for that! These books guide children to an understanding, that the weak, idiotic son of God, is a living hoax, who will be humiliated when the rain of fire comes... while we, his [Satan's] faithful servants, laugh and cavort in victory."** [64]

In Satanism we were taught that at the "final" battle—the Battle of Armageddon—Satan would defeat Jesus Christ, killing Him once and for all. Then, with his demons and the humans who serve him, Satan will assault the Throne of God and totally overthrow the Father, placing Satan on the Throne as God!

These are NOT isolated statements. Read what the High Priest and founder of the First Church of Satan wrote in *The Satanic Bible*:

> **"I dip my forefinger in the watery blood of your impotent mad redeemer, and write over his thorn-torn brow: TRUE prince of evil, the king of the slaves."** [65]

> **"I gaze into the glassy eye of your fearsome Jehovah,**

65

and pluck him by the beard. I uplift a broad-axe,
and open his worm-eaten skull!" [66]

"Behold the crucifix; what does it symbolize?
Pallid incompetence hanging on a tree." [67]

It might interest you to know, that even though LaVey was a defiant,
haughty and arrogant man, he died from heart complications, a weak,
sick, and beaten man.

The point is, when witches and Satanists are endorsing and praising
these books, **YOU KNOW THERE HAS TO BE SOMETHING
WRONG WITH THEM!**

The young "dabbler" is aided in their search and practice of occult magic through materials like these, and led to the "darker" practices....

UNDER THE SPELL OF HARRY POTTER

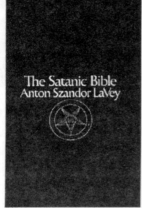

..through materials like these!

CHAPTER SIX
HARRY POTTER: THE MOVIE

In the fall of 1999, I heard a rumor that a major motion picture company was planning to turn the first book, *Harry Potter and the Sorcerer's Stone*, into a movie script.

That rumor, it seems, turned out to be true! As the story unfolded more in the entertainment magazines and in the news on the Internet, *Warner Brothers*, of *Time-Warner-AOL*, was in the process of securing the filming rights. Plans were to have auditions for parts in the U.S. and England, and at press time, a director for the movie has not yet been named, although Steven Speilberg, the famous director of *E.T.*, *Close Encounters Of The Third Kind*, the *Indiana Jones* series, as well as numerous other films, was being considered for that position.

According to *Entertainment Weekly,* the September 14, 2001 issue, there was an article on the Harry Potter movie. The article stated that in 1997, producer David Heyman (*Juice*, *Ravenous*) had just returned to London after a stint in Hollywood, in search of a children's book that would have a wide appeal as a movie. It seems his staff found the book, *Harry Potter and the Philosopher's Stone*, a then bestseller in England. Heyman's assistant read the book and pushed it. "It's a cool idea," Heyman recalls her saying. "It's about a boy in a wizarding school." Heyman immediately fell in love with this idea. He is quoted as saying,

> "It's such a human, moving tale. Harry is such an 'everybody'. He comes from a damaged home. He's not a great academic. Moreover, Hogwart's is a school that all of us would have wanted to go to. The book wasn't sentimental. It had an edge. It was wickedly funny. It was fiercely imaginative. Those were all the reasons I like it." [68]

UNDER THE SPELL OF HARRY POTTER

Heyman then contacted J.K. Rowling, and they struck up a friendship. It seems Ms. Rowling's biggest concern was that the movie would be true to the original story in the book. By now it was 1998, and Rowling's sequel, *Harry Potter and the Chamber of Secrets*, had been released. Heyman then pitched Harry Potter to Warner Brothers. Together, they reportedly offered $700,000 for both books and were accepted. They immediately began searching for the right screenwriter. Enter Steve Kloves, best known for his screen adaptation of *The Fabulous Baker Boys*. Kloves also met several times with author J.K. Rowling, first, to assure her that he would not "butcher" her baby, and second, to get input from Rowling for the movie's story lines.

The movie was originally scheduled to be shot in the U.S., but after two of Britain's top film industry officials flew to the U.S. and pleaded their case as to why the movie should be shot in England (the story takes place there), a decision was made to move the shooting to England. After offering Warner Brothers a package they couldn't refuse, the date for beginning to shoot the film was set. They had convinced Warner Brothers that such a movie had to be shot on a grand scale, and there was nowhere in the United States to do that or would do justice to the story they were putting on film.

It seems that Speilberg was working on three other projects at the time and was undecided which one would have first priority. Speilberg decided to go with the movie *A.I.* (Artificial Intelligence). With Speilberg out of the picture, Warner Brothers set out to look for a director who could begin right away, as they were attempting to get the final production wrapped up and in the theatres by October 2001, just in time for Halloween!

Those being considered included Rob Reiner, Wolfgang Peterson, Alan Parker, Terry Gilliam, Ivan Reitman, and Chris Columbus. During a two-hour audition, Columbus described what his adaptation would look like, and it fit the bill of what the company was looking for. Because the actors in the movie would be mostly children, Columbus was chosen for his previous successes with child actors. After all, he had directed *Home Alone* and *Bicentennial Man*, as well as written the screenplays for *Gremlins* and *Young Sherlock Holmes*. According to the

Entertainment Weekly article, Columbus wanted the entire cast to be British! In one of the director's meetings, Rowling was invited to sit in, and Columbus asked her to draw him a map of her "magical realm" to help him in production design. Rowling was included in the project as much as possible. **After all, who else understood so much about the world of witchcraft and wizardry?**

By the summer of 2000, the supporting cast had been chosen and announced: Maggie Smith would play the stern character, Professor McGonnagall; Richard Harris, long-time popular British actor, would play the part of Hogwart's Headmaster, Albus Dumbledore; Alan Rickman for the part of Professor Snape, and Robbie Coltrane as the school's blundering groundskeeper, Hagrid. The most difficult character to cast would be that of the boy wizard, Harry Potter. By July of 2000, an actor still had not been selected, and Warner Brothers was becoming nervous, as they wanted to begin the shooting by September. After hundreds of auditions, no child actor had fit the part. Then Columbus, who had seen a recent BBC production of *David Copperfield*, remembered he had been intrigued with the child actor, David Radcliffe. After Heyman and Kloves went to see this play, they contacted the young actor's parents and persuaded them to allow Radcliffe to play the part of Harry.

On August 21, 2000, the announcement was made that Radcliffe was Potter, and that newcomers Rupert Grint and Emma Watson would play the parts of Ron Weasley and Hermione Granger, Harry's school friends.

The staff of Heyman and Kloves, along with the British movie industry officials, had been busy scouring England's countryside for the "right" locations. Now comes the biggest blasphemy in this entire story: A site of holy worship for more than 1,300 years had been chosen to represent Hogwart's School of Witchcraft and Wizardry! Do you grasp the depths of that? Holy ground, where the worship of God takes place, is chosen to be turned into a school of witchcraft and sorcery for the production of the Harry Potter movie! The magnitude of this act is simply inconceivable!

The site chosen was England's Glouchester Cathedral, a place of worship, whose construction was ordered by William the Conqueror, and has the bones of King Edward II moldering within its walls. It is famous for its candy-colored stained glass and twisted stonework that makes visitors stop and gasp. The Very Reverend Nicholas Bury, Dean of Glouchester, had previously turned down "generous" offers from Warner Brothers for the rights to shoot the film there, due to what he had considered "the use of pagan imagery in the stories". However, after another meeting with the movie company, this stand taken by the good Reverend began to falter and finally fall. Afterwards, this same "man of God" issued a statement saying he had re-thought his stand on this matter and commented:

> **"Glouchester is one of the most beautiful cathedrals, and its friendliness and human scale have often been remarked upon. It is an atmospheric place, and good for a story about a boy making friends in his first year at school."** [69]

It is clear to me that the good Reverend apparently never picked up and read a Harry Potter book, nor did he realize the spiritual magnitude of letting a place of holy worship be used to represent a school teaching "unholy" practices!

According to *Charismanews.com*, Christian Internet company owners, Derek and Paula Clare led a protest over the Church of England's decision to allow scenes for the first Harry Potter movie to be shot at Glouchester Cathedral. Paula Clare told the *London Times*:

> **"As adults, we should be standing up to say that Witchcraft is wrong. Few people understand the spiritual realm, and its affect in our lives. There are only two spiritual powers, God and the devil, so if something is not of God, it is of the devil."** [70]

AMEN to that Sister! Praise God, some Christian brothers and sisters rallied and took a stand for Jesus in this matter—sadly though, not enough. Nick Bury, Dean of the Cathedral, said the Clares were overreacting. Calling the Potter books "splendid", he said:

> **"They emphasize that truth is better than lies, good overcomes evil, and the use of gifts should be responsible. They are extraordinarily wholesome books, and children should be encouraged to read them." [71]**

In my opinion, formed by the actions of these "men of God", THEY SOLD OUT TO THE DARK SIDE. What absolutely ludicrous and ridiculous statements!

Let's examine their reasoning together: First, Harry Potter wouldn't know the "truth" if it struck him right square in his face! Nor would his so-called friends, or should we call them "partners in crime"? As we have seen throughout the books, the young wizards and witches use lies to get themselves out of trouble, so what "truth" is Bury referring to? Second, he states that they overcome evil. While this may be a true statement, the means by which they overcome evil are spiritually unacceptable. They constantly use spells, conjuring, curses, necromancy, and other occult practices to fight evil. Once again, YOU **DO NOT** FIGHT **WITCHCRAFT** WITH **WITCHCRAFT!**

These men need to spend more time reading the Bible they are supposed to be preaching from when they are behind the pulpit. **Harry Potter is NOT A BIBLE;** yet, it seems many are trying to make it one by substituting this fantasy Witchcraft for the Word of God or make it fit into the Word of God. **IMPOSSIBLE!**

I couldn't wait to give you a Christian review of *Harry Potter and the Sorcerer's Stone* movie. All that was available for some time was information posted in entertainment magazines, the Internet, and movie trailers. Without having to actually go to the movies, you may view these trailers on the excellent *Jeremiah Films* video titled *Harry Potter: Witchcraft Repackaged*, which is a well-done production featuring commentary from best-selling Christian authors Robert S. McGee and Caryl Matrisciana. The video contains actual film footage of Witchcraft rituals, an exploration of the rise of interest in Witchcraft, and the point made repeatedly that Witchcraft, no matter what form it may be in, is NOT wholesome, NOT moral, and that the Harry Potter books are NOT good or okay for our children. You may view a sample of this video by going to the website; www.therealpotter.com, and clicking on the video's trailer link. You may also order the complete video through The Prophecy Club® at (785) 266-1112.

For almost four years now, children of all ages, from everywhere have been dreaming of wizards, gimlet-eyed goblins, terrible trolls, unicorns, dragons, letter-bearing owls, ghosts, whispering serpents, flying broomsticks, magic wands, spells, potions, and terrifying shapes of evil. Their worst nightmares have now arrived. Their wait to enter into a magic land, where children are the masters, is over! The Harry Potter movie was released in the U.S. and Canada on November 16, 2001.

There was an interesting rumor circulating on the Internet that Warner

Brothers had stepped up its premiere release in London to November 5, 2001. If this rumor were true, then it would also fall on the celebration of Guy Fawkes Day (the man who plotted to blow up Parliament and stop the translation and printing of the King James Bible). This indeed was the actual release date set for the England.

I can be certain of one thing, this movie will be **THE** top-selling movie of the year, as well as a best-seller and most widely rented video when it is finally released in that form. It will be the Number One attraction, and its proceeds will far excel that of any other movie put out for the rest of this year, or for that matter, any movie last year!

It is reported that the film contains over 600 special effects shots, handled by a variety of F/X industries. Industrial Light & Magic Company is producing the Voldemort character, who is so horrifying that he must be computer animated, rather than played by an actor!

In anticipation of the U.S. release of *Harry Potter and The Sorcerer's Stone* movie, even *Vanity Fair* magazine, in its October 2001 issue, had a 22-page tribute to the movie, complete with photos of the actors and scenes from the movie.

Harry Potter fans packed 200 theaters across Britain and Ireland last March just to watch the first 107-second trailer. Internet surfers in over 150 countries logged on to the Warner Brothers website to see it. I believe that this movie will also be the biggest catalyst in boosting the interest in witchcraft and other occult practices that we have seen! It will promote the interest of children worldwide and make them want to learn more about how they, too, can be like their favorite book character, and now Witchcraft movie star, HARRY POTTER.

Students at Hogwart's listen intensely, as a Professor instructs the class in the art of levitation. Here we see Hermione using a magic wand to make a feather rise into the air.

Harry and a friend venture through the "Magic Forest", a place filled with mystery and "terrifying monsters".

Professor Albus Dumbledore, Grand Wizard, and Headmaster of Hogwart's School of Wizardry & Witchcraft.

Harry arrives at the train station with his "familiar", a white owl, symbol of "white" witchcraft.

The shrewd and stern "old school" witchcraft teacher, Professor McGonagal.

UNDER THE SPELL OF HARRY POTTER

Thanks to my stepson Adam, who works at the local theater, I was able to view a private screening of *Harry Potter and the Sorcerer's Stone* shown to employees and their families. My wife, Jo Ann, and I looked forward to viewing this hyped-up movie. During the afternoon, I had telephoned a minister friend of mine, William Schnoebelen, author of *Lucifer Dethroned* and several other books exposing the occult. I told him that the emblem used for Hogwart's school also contained some words in Latin. I asked him if he could assist me by translating these words. He was not available at the time, so I left a message. Just as I was about to leave the house to meet my stepson and wife at the theater, I received a call from Bill. He told me the translation of the Latin words was: "NEVER TICKLE A SLEEPING DRAGON."

At first I found this amusing, but as I thought more about these words, I begin to see a more sinister meaning! Satan, the enemy of mankind, is referred to as the Dragon in scripture. If you tickle a sleeping dragon and he wakes you are facing an ANGRY monster! Could it be that the "sleeping dragon" here is a symbol for the "hidden" witchcraft in Harry Potter? On the previous page is the emblem of Hogwart's, complete with the seals of the four schools and the Latin terminology. What could this "sleeping dragon" be? In the Harry Potter books, dragons are considered dangerous creatures, not fit to live among the wizards and witches. In the movie, Hagrid (the giant) receives a dragon egg and hatches a baby dragon. He wants to keep the it and raise it, but it is soon revealed that he is hiding a dragon, and Dumbledore confiscates it and sends it to Romania.

The movie opens with baby Harry being placed at the doorstep of the Dursley's, Harry's only surviving family, by Dumbledore and Professor McGonagle, to be raised by them until he reaches his eleventh birthday. After Hagrid finally confronts Harry and tells him that he is a powerful wizard, Harry chooses to leave the Dursley's, (who had him basically imprisoned and was enslaved by them) and leaves for Hogwart's. At one point in the movie, Harry and the Dursley's visit a zoo, where Dudley Dursley antagonizes a huge python snake, trying to get its attention. As soon as Harry touches the glass cage, the snake takes notice, perks up, and begins to communicate with Harry. Here, Harry also "wishes" that the glass would disappear, and as it does, Dudley falls into the cage but is unharmed as the snake thanks Harry and escapes.

As Hagrid takes Harry to Diagon Alley, a marketplace for wizards and witches, Harry begins to pick up "school" supplies, including a magic wand. After trying several wands with disastrous results, the shopkeeper brings out a special wand. He tells Harry that there were two wands made with the feather of a Phoenix. One belonged to a wizard who used the magic for good, and the other belonged to the brother who gave Harry the scar, Who's-Name-Must-Not-Be-Spoken (Voldemort). As the wand is placed in Harry's hand, a gush of wind comes upon them and they can feel the power surging. Clearly, this wand once belonged to Harry's father.

UNDER THE SPELL OF HARRY POTTER

As Harry enters Hogwart's, the setting is very elaborate and resembles what one would perceive as a school for Witchcraft and Wizardry. The special effects are very well done, and the flying broom and Quidditch scenes are breathtaking.

There were many exciting exploits undertaken by Harry, Ron, and Hermione, all done under the cover of night. Harry and his friends break many of the rules established by Hogwart's, but instead of being reprimanded (because Harry is "special") these infractions are overlooked. In one scene, Professor McGonagle even presents Harry with a streamlined broomstick, known as the Nimbus 2000! He also receives a cloak, which allows him to become invisible and move about Hogwart's undetected. There are also many scary scenes, where the children confront several monsters, including a three-headed dog, vines that crush you to death (known as The Devil's Snare), huge chess pieces that move on voice-command and will attack your chess piece with huge swords and other weapons as you are riding on the piece, and the evil Lord Voldemort himself, who is computer animated and first introduced as he drinks the blood of a unicorn in order to stay alive and "immortal". Voldemort is living and hiding inside Professor Quirrel, one of the school's instructors, who is loyal to his master. This clearly depicts demonic possession.

Another interesting scene shows the school getting ready for and celebrating Yule, referring to Christmastime. Here we see one of the creatures of Hogwart's decorating a tree with a crescent moon and star ornament. (See chapter on symbols.)

The most striking scenes come at the end of the movie, as Voldemort and Quirrel are trying to get the Sorcerer's Stone from Harry. Voldemort, whose face is now the backside of Professor Quirrel's head, tells Harry that he wants him to join the "dark side" (Star Wars). Harry refuses, and Voldemort tells Harry that there is no good or evil, only power, and those too weak to seek it. Harry is also told that the power he possesses is expelled through his skin. Harry is attacked by Quirrel, who tries to strangle him. As Harry grabs Quirrel's hand, it becomes badly burned. Then Harry touches his face, and it too becomes burned and turns to cinders and ashes. (Quirrel had once told Harry not to touch him.) In the background, we see Voldemort becoming something that resembles smoke, slithering up the stairway and out of sight. As Harry is seen recuperating, Dumbledore tells Harry that the reason that Quirrel was burned by his touch was because the power he transmitted through his touch was love, the love given him by the sacrifice made by his mother in giving her life to save Harry from Voldemort.

After we returned home and were discussing the movie, Jo Ann told me her concerns about it. She pointed out that she prayed that the statement about the power of love being transmitted by touch would not influence children to believe that they could transmit things through touch. She also pointed out that in the story the children made things happen through voice-command, and she saw a danger of making children believe that they were in command; thus taking away parental authority, giving the child control and expecting the parent to be led by their children's "desires" by commanding, not asking, for things.

The important point to make here is that the movie was definitely entertaining, exciting, and had great special effects, but, as we were leaving the theater, I turned to Jo Ann and said, "If this movie doesn't make kids want to study this stuff more, go deeper, and make them think that being a witch or wizard is exciting and fun, then I don't know what will." She sadly agreed. Rowling got her wish, the movie stayed very true to the book.

Warner Brothers has already begun work on the next movie, *Harry Potter and the Chamber Of Secrets*, scheduled for release in November of next year. They plan on doing a Harry Potter movie each year, until the seven book series has been completed. Then, what other Satanic devices will we have to look forward to?

UNDER THE SPELL OF HARRY POTTER

CHAPTER SEVEN
THE MERCHANDISING OF MAGIC

Already there are trailers appearing on television in the form of commercials, billboards, trading card games, video games, toys, and a mega-million-dollar marketing campaign from Coca-Cola promoting the new *Harry Potter and the Sorcerer's Stone* movie, with the promise of more Harry Potter merchandise to come. Around Christmas of last year, while my wife, Jo Ann, and I were shopping in a large mall, we viewed a massive display of Harry Potter merchandise in one of the Warner Brothers stores.

As we entered the store, we were both floored at the shelves of Harry Potter merchandise! Most of it was promotional material for the upcoming movie. There were Harry Potter backpacks, toy figures, magical stones, and T-shirts galore. I was particularly shocked to overhear a young mother asking her daughter, who was approximately seven or eight years old, "Now honey, which shirt do you want? Do you want the one with Harry flying on a broomstick, or do you want this one with the big lightning bolt?" The shirt she was inquiring about was a black T-shirt with a large yellow lightning bolt on the front, symbolizing Harry's magical scar he received from his first encounter with the evil Voldemort. The staff were all wearing black T-shirts advertising **Hogwart's School of Wizardry and Witchcraft!**

My wife informed me that the place was giving her a headache so we left. We were impressed to pray outside the store for all the small children and youth who were being deceived by the Harry Potter phenomenon, and were purchasing mememorabilia of their favorite Harry Potter characters. We began to see the magic in the merchandising of Harry Potter. Just like the books, these articles were designed to boost the interest of youth in witchcraft!

With the release of the new Harry Potter movie, the Mattel Toy Company has purchased the exclusive rights to produce the Potter paraphernalia, and have launched a Harry Potter merchandising campaign all across America—just in time for Halloween 2001. The *Harry Potter and the Sorcerer's Stone* soundtrack CD, featuring music and sounds from the movie, is scheduled to hit the shelves on October 30th.

Mattel Toys has produced and released a line of Harry Potter action figures. Notice how this figure of Harry is not only dressed in wizard robes and sporting a magic wand, but also has a collectible piece that comes with it, which also happens to have the seal of witchcraft, the goddess Diana (crescent moon and star) engraved on it.

THE MERCHANDISING OF MAGIC

This Harry Potter figure is supposed to be Harry, dressed in gear and ready to play Quidditch, a polo type of game, played on "flying" broomsticks.

This next Mattel toy figure features our young hero wizard soaring above Hogwart's on his Firebolt magic broomstick.

UNDER THE SPELL OF HARRY POTTER

The avid Potter fan can track the new year with this calendar featuring a scene from the *Harry Potter and the Sorcerer's Stone* movie. The young star of Harry Potter is played by actor Daniel Radcliffe seen in this photo.

This Harry Potter coin is actually legal tender on the Isle of Man.

Harry Potter "magic" puzzles and Potter Trivia games have also appeared nationwide on the market and are available at local toy and bookstores.

Also available on the market are Harry Potter UNO cards. These cards replace the "boring", traditional UNO cards of old!

One of the most popular sales items is the Harry Potter Trading Card Game, which is played much the same way the Pokemon Trading Card Game is played. Each character has special "powers", and the player can either gain points and more powers, or lose points and weaken the power strength of his opponent, by casting spells and using curses.

The object of the game, as in Pokemon, is to become the "Master" (wizard). Oh yes, these cards are manufactured by *Wizards of the Coast*, the same company which produces and distributes the Pokemon, Magic: The Gathering, and other occult trading card games.

A young wizard or witch can keep track of his/her activities and spell-casting with the Harry Potter Journal pictured here.

The online mega-bookstore, Amazon.com, lists Harry Potter books on its website. When one goes to check into a book's availability or to get a description of a book, the buyer is shown other books related to the one he/she is inquiring about. For instance, when a buyer goes to this site to order *Harry Potter and the Sorcerer's Stone*, another link is provided for a "companion" book. The buyer of this book, for example, is led to an even more in-depth occult book entitled *The Sorcerer's Companion*: *A Guide to the Magical World*.

Another link and click of the computer mouse takes the reader to a book called *Magical Worlds of Harry Potter*.

Inside the book, the reader can look up terms, descriptions, and meanings to the creatures found in the Potter books, as if they were "real" and existing now!

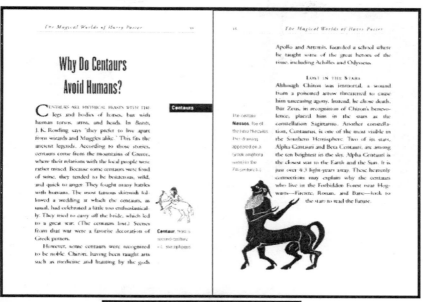

UNDER THE SPELL OF HARRY POTTER

Another popular item with the children is the Harry Potter Stickerbook, where the child can peel off the sticker, place it on a schoolbook or notebook, or even paste the sticker on their forehead as is done with the popular "lightning bolt".

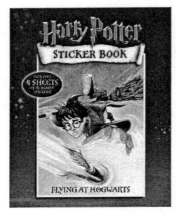

As you can see, the book and toy producers have gone out of their way to make sure that any item containing the picture, or name of Harry Potter is widely available. With them, there are no limits!

CHAPTER EIGHT
THE REAL DANGER OF
HARRY POTTER

I believe, that during my extensive study of the Harry Potter phenomenon, the Lord revealed the REAL plan of the enemy. I believe He showed how there is more to Harry Potter than meets the eye, and that He has revealed some of Satan's vital, strategic plans. I would like to share those revelations with you now, to better equip you in combatting this assault on our children and the God-ordained family unit itself.

As we have seen, there are numerous comments from educators, librarians, politicians, Christian leaders, and even children and parents supporting the argument that the Harry Potter books alone are not enough to make our children into witches, Satanists, or other occult practitioners. I have to say at this point, that I agree. The Harry Potter books alone ARE NOT enough to turn our children into practitioners of the "craft". However, I believe they are the "hook" or "lure" that will promote an unhealthy fascination with the higher forms of the occult practices described in the Potter books. I also believe that the REAL practitioners are using the books to do just that!

Once the child has read a Harry Potter book and been introduced into a "magical world" where he/she is the master and ruler of their own destiny, they begin to crave more. As they read of Harry and his friend's terrifying adventures, they become more "connected" to him, feeling that Harry is much like them, a "nobody" who is subject to strict and unfair family rules. When they see how Harry broke away from being under family rules and regulations, and was no longer subject to any parental authority, they begin to want to be "just like" their hero. When they begin to read how Harry and his friends lie, cheat, steal, and generally rebel against authority, and how, instead of being punished or reprimanded for such disobedience, they are instead rewarded and praised, they begin to feel, "This is the way it should be in my life." When they have been introduced to the casting of spells to get revenge on an enemy or the making of potions in order to gain control over someone else, they get more interested in this world of witchcraft and wizardry.

They begin to wonder just how fun it would be to be able to soar through the air on a flying broomstick or wave a magic wand and watch things they desire materialize before their very eyes. They begin to wonder what it would be like to communicate with the spirits of dead loved ones or friends who have died. They also wonder what it would be like to face an evil being so terrible you could not even look upon it, to battle it, and have victory over it. Indeed, Harry Potter has whetted their appetites for more!

In fact, two large companies and merchandising conglomerates, Coca-Cola and Mattel Toys, have gotten behind the media and merchandising promotions for the movie. The Coca-Cola Company began promoting the movie, with its introduction of collectible Harry Potter Coke cans, in early October, 2001. Mattel Toys purchased the rights for production and distribution of Harry Potter figures and other paraphernalia. Huge amounts of Potter products can be easily found in local bookstores and Warner Brothers stores.

In classrooms, as well as homes all over the country, personal computers are being used more and more by students and family members. One of the greatest tools used to acquire information is the Internet. You can find just about anything by going to your browser and typing in what you are searching for—even witchcraft web pages! The Internet is overflowing with home websites for groups of all different beliefs and religions. A personal search I have done at home turned up hundreds of high-profile websites, offering everything from how to cast spells and curses, to how to perform actual occult rituals, just by getting online. In fact, I have no problem tapping into The Church of Satan website, where you have an opportunity to apply for church membership right on the site itself! On one of the sites, called "The Witches' Voice", you have an opportunity to chat with and receive instruction in the "craft" from actual witches. Another site dealt with Demonology and even gave instructions on how to summon the denizens of hell! Imagine, your child and almost any other child has the same opportunity to find these sites. In a recent Internet search for Harry Potter references, I found more than 600,000 links that take you to related websites.

There is even a Warner Brothers *Harry Potter and the Sorcerer's Stone* movie website, where a child can go and be offered the opportunity to sign up at Hogwart's online!

So, here is Satan's plan: You whet the appetites of children who are confused and not quite grounded in family morals, values, and standards (especially those young enough not fully grounded in their faith in Jesus) and introduce them to Harry Potter, a boy wizard who learns and practices the art of Witchcraft and Sorcery. You then bolster their interest in these practices and instill in them the idea that there is no good or evil, only magic, and that it's okay to practice Witchcraft, because it is a moral, wholesome thing to do, as well as the fact that you will receive a reward from it. Finally, when their interest in these practices is at its highest peak, offer the use of the Internet, which is exploding with information that is theirs for the taking, and teaches them how they too **can be just like Harry Potter!** From what the Lord has shown me thus far, I believe this is the strategy Satan is using to recruit our children into his ranks! Our enemy is very cunning, clever, and extremely sneaky. He comes through the "back door" so to speak, rather than coming at us with a "frontal" assault, as this would definitely give his plans away.

J. K. Rowling herself has expressed surprise at the volume of mail she receives from young readers, writing to her as if Hogwart's were real and wanting to know how they might enter the school and become witches and wizards themselves.

Here are just a few examples of comments made by ordinary children— ones who think it's "cool" to be a practitioner of occult magic:

"I wish I could do magic. Not just like making people rise up into the air, but real magic, like turning them into newts and frogs, and making people do something, or stop doing something. I'd love to have a Unicorn for a pet. I was sorry there wasn't more about Unicorns in the book. They're really beautiful, and magical. The only Unicorn in the book was killed, and Voldemort drank its blood to make him stronger." —Shanti, 13 years old

"Mysteries and magic are wonderful. I liked it when Harry and his friends got into trouble because they were using magic—like when Harry played tricks on his cousin Dudley, and blew up Aunt Marge. I especially like Lord Voldemort and Sirius Black." —Daniel, 9 years old

"I'd recommend the books to fifth and sixth graders. They're fun, exciting, not too slow or shallow, with funny characters. I liked it when the bad guys were in the woods, and killed the Unicorn and Voldemort drank its blood, but they got stopped by the Centaurs, and Harry watched the whole thing." —Julie, 13 years old

"My favorite character is Hermione, not just because she's a girl like me, but because she helps Harry and Ron get into stuff. I'd like to go to wizard school, learn magic, and put spells on people. I'd make up an ugly spell, and then, it's payback time! I'd turn people into witches with big warts on their faces, with two little hairs sticking out in different directions." —Catherine, 9 years old

"I would like to go to wizardry school, because it would be really different from normal school and it would be like getting a taste of a totally different culture, more like the world we live in." —Emma, 12 years old

"What's neat about the magic is the things in jars, and the dark, dirty chambers, with toads everywhere, and the rats. And the spells, I'd like to turn someone into a frog. I'd like to turn myself into a dog, I really like dogs." —Perrin, 9 years old

Now, imagine your horror as a parent, when you realize that your child has clicked into a website where practitioners of the occult arts are waiting, willing, and ready to give him/her instructions in how to do things like these and worse...FOR REAL!

View this picture for a few moments. Most readers will notice the woman in a seductive pose, but not notice she is a witch standing in front of a satanic pentagram. Our children are being seduced into seeing Harry Potter as "cute" and "fun" and not seeing the **EVIL** behind it!

UNDER THE SPELL OF HARRY POTTER

CHAPTER NINE
WHAT CAN BE DONE
ABOUT HARRY ?

By now, if you are a parent, you are probably gasping and grabbing your head with both hands asking, "What can I do about all this?"

The first and most important thing to do is **REPENT**! That's right, we are the ones who allowed this abomination into our homes. Children, especially young ones, don't have the money to go out and buy these books. It is we, the adults, who buy the books for them or give them to other children as presents! God has established an order for the family unit, and He has set an awesome responsibility before us: to bring up our children in Him, the TRUE Father. We have to remember that our children do not "belong" to us. They are God's children, and He has placed them in our care to raise and nurture.

We need to repent for allowing witchcraft to be brought into that family structure, then turn from it and get it OUT of our homes and the lives of our children.

PRAY- We have to remember that we are not fighting a flesh and blood enemy, but as Ephesians 6 tells us, we are battling principalities, powers, rulers of the darkness of this world, and spiritual wickedness in high places.

2 Corinthians 10:4-5 *"(For the weapons of our warfare are not carnal, but mighty through God to the pulling down of strong holds;) Casting down imaginations, and every high thing that exalteth itself against the knowledge of God, and bringing into captivity every thought to the obedience of Christ."*

We must stand in our God-given authority, through the power of God's Holy Spirit, and intercede for the children who have been lured into and are now captive to this world of witchcraft and sorcery. We even need to pray and intercede for J. K. Rowling, that the Lord will open her eyes to see the very real danger in the books she is writing. We need to come against these forces boldly and without wavering. We must take a stand for our Lord, His Word, what is right, and CONTINUE STANDING until we have the victory!

SUPPORT - We must support those ministers and ministries that are working to expose these evils with our prayers and financial support. These are the ones standing boldly on the front lines of the battle, and the ones whom the enemy "hits" the most!

ORGANIZE - Harry Potter got into our schools and into our homes because a lot of "well-meaning" Christians sat idly by and let it happen! We need to organize. There is power in numbers, especially if those numbers are God's people. We are the ones who need to be going into the schools and demanding they remove the Harry Potter books from their libraries and curriculum. While on The Prophecy Club® tour, I had many mothers come to me with tears in their eyes, telling me that their child had been "required" to read Harry Potter in their school.

It's time to tell these educators that even if my child receives an "F" for refusing to read the Harry Potter books, so be it! Go into the bookstores, and in a courteous, but firm way, voice your feelings about the books to the store Manager. Better yet, take a church group or Bible study group of Spirit-filled Christian brothers and sisters, go to the occult section of the store, and proceed to lay hands on and command the spells and powers over those books to be broken in the name of **Jesus of Nazareth**. (This really works!) Then, proceed to the children's section and do the same over every book God shows you to take authority over—especially the Harry Potter books!

EDUCATE - Give out copies of this book, and other materials exposing the Harry Potter phenomenon, to school administrators and officials, as well as other parents, church Pastors, and youth leaders. We **must** also **make sure** that our particular church **does not** condone or promote Harry Potter, and that they take a firm stand against Witchcraft, Satanism, and other occult practices—including the observance of Halloween.

WRITE - Write to these "Christian" leaders who have told us that Harry Potter is not the "real" kind of witchcraft spoken of in God's Word. Tell them that the Lord sees it differently! Share with them the knowledge you have acquired. Many of them speak but are unaware of the truth.

BOYCOTT - We must boycott any company or store promoting Harry Potter materials; especially Coca-Cola, Mattel Toys, and Warner Brothers stores. Scholastic, Inc. is the exclusive publisher of the Rowling books and are the ones responsible for getting the Harry Potter series, along with other stories of witchcraft and the supernatural, into our schools. This organization supplies the majority of reading materials to our schools and reaches over 40 million children a year. Teachers are encouraged to read the materials aloud to the class. They have "vowed" to keep Harry Potter alive in the school systems and to promote this, and other questionable material, in the U.S., Canada, and ultimately internationally. Finally...

KEEP WATCH - If the Potter phenomenon isn't as successful as they hope it will be, "other" Satanic devices will come forth, each more enticing than its predecessor. The witches and Satanists have used Harry Potter to successfully recruit youth into their ranks, but it won't stop there.

Children are sensitive, curious little creatures, who are ready to "bite" at anything that captivates, excites, and motivates them or offers "another" or "better" way of living. They find it difficult enough just to be themselves! They are often confused and not able to make informed, morally correct decisions. They are dependent upon us as adults to have careful discernment on their behalf in the area of culture, because they do not have the knowledge and experience that comes with age. They are easily deceived, very impressionable, and form opinions and beliefs at an early age. They are not yet capable of distinguishing between "right" from "wrong" and "good" from "evil". They rely on **US** to teach them these things. They rely on **US** to teach them the **TRUTH** about everything. They rely on **US** to teach them about Jesus and His great love. Ultimately, they rely on **US** to teach them **THE TRUTH ABOUT HARRY POTTER AND BREAK THE SPELL!**

ENDNOTES:

1. J. K. Rowling, *Harry Potter and the Goblet of Fire*, Scholastic, Inc., p. 14
2. Ibid, p. 15
3. Ibid, p. 15
4. Ibid
5. "Interview with J. K. Rowling", *http://www.scholastic.com*
6. Ibid
7. Ibid
8. "J. K. Rowling", *LIFE Magazine*, November 1999
9. Ibid
10. "Interview with J. K. Rowlings", *BOOKS LINK Magazine*
11. Ibid
12. Ibid
13. J. K. Rowling, *Harry Potter and the Sorcerer's Stone*, Scholastic Inc., 1998
14. Ibid, p. 302
15. Starhawk, *Spiral Dance*
16. J. K. Rowling, *Harry Potter and the Sorcerer's Stone*, Scholastic Inc., 1998
17. Ibid
18. Ibid
19. J. K. Rowling, *Harry Potter and the Prisoner of Azkaban*, Scholastic Inc.
20. J. K. Rowling, *Harry Potter and the Chamber of Secrets*, Scholastic Inc., p. 228
21. J. K. Rowling, *Harry Potter and the Goblet of Fire*, Scholastic, Inc., p. 712
22. J. K. Rowling, *Harry Potter and the Chamber of Secrets*, Scholastic Inc., p. 166
23. J. K. Rowling, *Harry Potter and the Goblet of Fire*, Scholastic, Inc., p. 33
24. Ibid, pp. 229, 443, 456, 577, 581

25. J. K. Rowling, *Harry Potter and the Chamber of Secrets,* Scholastic Inc., p. 57

26. Ibid, p.100

27. Ibid, p. 62

28. Ibid, p. 319

29. Ibid, p. 444

30. J. K. Rowling, *Harry Potter and the Goblet of Fire,* Scholastic, Inc., pp. 88, 117

31. J. K. Rowling, *Harry Potter and the Chamber of Secrets,* Scholastic Inc., p. 200

32. Ibid, p. 232

33. Ibid, p. 546

34. "Interview with J. K. Rowling", *http://www.cbc4kids.ca*

35. "Interview with J. K. Rowling", *http://www.amazon.com/ harrypotterbooks.html*

36. "Interview with J. K. Rowling", *http://www.cbc4kids.ca*

37. "Interview with Ashley Daniels", *The Onion Newsletter*, July 2000

38. High Priest Egan, First Church of Satan. http:// www.churchofsatan.com

39. J. K. Rowling, *Harry Potter and the Chamber of Secrets,* Scholastic Inc., p. 196

40. Ibid, pp.91-92

41. Ibid, pp. 92-93

42. J. K. Rowling, *Harry Potter and the Sorcerer's Stone,* Scholastic Inc., 1998, p. 292

43. *A Witches' Bible*, p. 141

44. Anton Szandor LaVey, *The Satanic Bible*, Avon Publishing

45. J. K. Rowling, *Harry Potter and the Sorcerer's Stone,* Scholastic Inc., 1998, p. 298

46. Ibid, p. 309

47. Ibid, p. 298

48. "Interview with Malcom Jones, *NEWSWEEK Magazine*, October 2000

49. Ted Olsen, *Christianity Today Magazine*, November 1999

50. Chuck Colson, *Breakpoint Radio Broadcast*, November 2, 1999
51. Dr. James Dobson, *Focus On The Family Radio*
52. Roy Maynard, *World Magazine*, May 22, 1999
53. Ibid, October 30, 1999
54. Mark Greene, *The British Christianity Magazine*
55. "Witches and Muggles", *Christian Century Magazine*, December 1, 1999
56. Ted Olsen, *Christianity Today Magazine*, November 1999
57. Alan Jacobs, Professor at Wheaton College
58. John Monk, *The State In Columbia*
59. "Interview with a spokesperson for the Pagan Federation, *NEWSWEEK Magazine*
60. Ibid
61. *Internet*
62. Jessica Lehman, *Internet*
63. Bradley Winters, *Internet*
64. Ibid
65. Anton Szandor LaVey, *The Satanic Bible*, Avon Publishing, p.30
66. Ibid
67. Ibid, p.31
68. "Interview with David Heyman", *Entertainment Weekly Magazine*, September 14, 2001
69. Very Reverend Nicholas Bury, Dean of Glouchester
70. Derek and Paula Clare, *http://charismanews.com*
71. Nick Bury,

UNDER THE SPELL OF HARRY POTTER

RESOURCES

Harry Potter and the Chamber of Secrets /J.K. Rowling / Scholastic Inc.

Harry Potter and the Prisoner of Azkaban / J.K. Rowling / Scholastic Inc.

Harry Potter and the Goblet of Fire / J.K. Rowling / Scholastic Inc.

Entertainment Weekly Magazine / July 1, 2000

http://www.Scholastic.com / Interview with J.K. Rowling

LIFE Magazine / November, 1999 issue

http://www.guyfawkes.com / guy fawkes day

The Onion Newsletter / July, 2000 issue

Witchcraft, Magic & Alchemy / Grillot de Givry

Spence's Encyclopedia of Occultism; Nicolas Flamel

Teen Witch / Silver Ravenwolf / Llewellyn Publications

The Satanic Bible / Anton Szandor LaVey/ Avon Publishing

Newsweek Magazine / October 2000 issue

Christianity Today Magazine / November 1999 issue

World Magazine / May 22, 1999, October 30, 1999 issues

UNDER THE SPELL OF HARRY POTTER

Breakpoint radio broadcast / Chuck Colson / November 2, 1999
Christian Century Magazine / December 1, 1999 issue

Time Magazine / December 17, 2000 issue

Entertainment Weekly Magazine / September 14, 2001 issue

http://www.Charismanews.com

VANITY FAIR Magazine / October, 2001 issue

http://www.warnerbros.com/ harry potter.html

http://www.mattel.com/harrypotter

http://www.Amazon.com/harrypotterbooks.html

Harry Potter and the Sorcerer's Stone movie / NewLine Cinema
Prod. / Warner Bros. Pictures/ Time / AOL

Photographs, other than bookcovers, toys, and movie posters were
acquired by anonymous sources as they came into my office before,
and while writing this book.

ADDITIONAL RESOURCES

If you liked the book *Under the Spell of Harry Potter* you will love the 2 hour and 40 minute illustrated video for a gift of $25.

The Occult in Your Living Room is another great video by Stephen Dollins, who was an ex-satanist High Priest for seven years with Anton LaVey's Church of Satan. He gives his personal testimony of how the power and love of Jesus Christ delivered him from the dark world. He exposes the subtle devices used to infiltrate the homes of Christians and non-Christians alike to lure the young and old into the practice of witchcraft and satanism. Discover the evil truth behind the Ouija board, astrology, Tarot cards, psychics, as well as today's crazes; movies, video games, role-playing fantasy games. Learn about devices used to initiate our children into the world of the occult by making evil appear "cute", such as: Halloween, Teletubbies, Pokemon and the children's book, *Harry Potter*. You will learn the evil meaning of symbols used by practitioners of Black Magic, as well as see these symbols used in modern jewelry. Stephen exposes the subliminal messages used in today's Rock music, and much more! Two - 2 hour and 40 minute video set for a gift of $40.

UNDER THE SPELL OF HARRY POTTER

Exposing the Illuminati from Within is a video by Bill Schnoebelen who was a Satanic and Voodoo High Priest, 2nd degree Church of Satan, New Age guru, occultist, channeler, 90th degree Mason, Knight Templar, and a member of the Illuminati. He taught astrology, Tarot cards, and astral projection. Bill shows how the conspiracy works and how it uses the Lodge and the highest echelons of power and technology from secret "black project" operations to form a world government. Two - 2 hour video set for a gift of $40.

The Light Behind Masonry, by Bill Schnoebelen, exposes the truth behind the secret "club" known as Freemasonry. A large percentage of Masons are kept in the dark on purpose so the real agenda can be carried out. Bill exposes the real intentions behind the images put forth by the Masons and Shriners. He tells about the secret signals, handshakes, meanings behind the clothing worn by each member and how they are blaspheming God and swearing allegiance to pagan gods. This video could save a loved one caught in the lie and lead them to true salvation. One 2-1/2 hour video for a gift of $25.

Satan's Art of Deception, by Tom Schumpert, exposes the deception of Satan through the snares of the New Age movement. Tom formerly taught hypnotic regression, aura reading, balancing, meditation and many other deceptions Satan uses to blind the people to the truth of Jesus Christ. Tom shares his testimony, exposes the many lies of other "religions" and how we can recognize the occult connections in our modern society. If you have loved ones in these modern deceptions, Tom will give you insights on how to reach them with the Truth! One 2 hour and 40 minute video for a gift of $25.

Six Hours In Heaven is a presentation by Henry Gruver, who walks you across flowers that sing the praises of the Father and a flowing robe that sings the righteousness of the saints. His 27-minute death experience gives comfort and reassurance to the redeemed of the Lord. This 2-1/2 hr. video feels like it lasts about 30 minutes! You can receive this for a gift of $25.

Wake Up America is the video of Dumitru Duduman. He was a Romanian pastor who

smuggled Bibles into Romania and Russia for 30 years. He was arrested and tortured five months, culminating with his being placed on the electric chair twice. He was sent to warn America. "It will start with an internal revolution in America, started by the Communists. Then from the oceans, Russia, Cuba, Nicaragua, Mexico, Central America, and two other nations will attack America." The nuclear missiles will land in California, Las Vegas, New York, and Florida. One 2 hour video for a gift of $25.

UNDER THE SPELL OF HARRY POTTER

Secrets of the Illuminati is a presentation by Dr. Stan Montieth, who is an international speaker on Geopolitics and his radio programs are heard around the world. In this video he reveals the shadow rulers who cause wars and revolutions, and explains the covert motivation of those working to create world government with special emphasis on the "Rhodes Scholar" secret society which Cecil Rhodes created in 1891. Dr. Monteith explains the spiritual forces that have energized the world revolutionary movement since its inception, and reveals the little known story of the true origin of communism and socialism. One 2 hour and 40 minute video for a gift of $25.

Final Steps to the New World Order is a video featuring Dr. Michael Coffman, Ph.D., who explains through global deception, intrigue and war how the world government is being formed right before our very eyes—what the UN has done to implement World Government, the consequences of World Government and how the EU, Russia and China are reducing American power. One 2 hour and 40 minute video for a gift of $25.

Send Check or Money Order to:
The Prophecy Club®
Box 750234
Topeka, KS 66675
Phone orders: 785/266-1112 • Fax: 785/266-6200
Quantity discounts are available.